# America's ★ Best
## BRAND-NAME RECIPES®

## *Fix it Quick*
# Comfort Food
## COOKBOOK

America's ★ Best
**BRAND-NAME RECIPES®**

**Pictured on the front cover:** Scalloped Chicken & Pasta *(page 162).*

**Pictured on the back cover** *(clockwise from top left):* Vegetable Pizza *(page 176),* Easy Citrus Berry Shortcake *(page 268)* and Crispy Oven-Baked Chicken *(page 102).*

ISBN: 0-8487-2869-6

Library of Congress Control Number: 2004102743

Manufactured in China.

8 7 6 5 4 3 2 1

**Microwave Cooking:** Microwave ovens vary in wattage. Use the cooking times as guidelines and check for doneness before adding more time.

**Preparation/Cooking Times:** Preparation times are based on the approximate amount of time required to assemble the recipe before cooking, baking, chilling or serving. These times include preparation steps such as measuring, chopping and mixing. The fact that some preparations and cooking can be done simultaneously is taken into account. Preparation of optional ingredients and serving suggestions is not included.

# Table of Contents

# Introduction

*You don't cook like your mother did, because preparing meals from scratch takes time you don't have. These days sitting down to share a satisfying home-cooked meal often seems like a challenge rather than a pleasure. America's Best Brand Name Fix It Quick Comfort Foods is just what you need to change that. With the right recipes and a little planning, your family can eat well even on the busiest days.*

## FIVE-INGREDIENT MAGIC

All of the recipes in this cookbook have five main ingredients or less, minimizing the amount of time spent chopping, slicing and measuring. It also means less time shopping and, in most cases, less time cooking and cleaning up. A few ingredients, such as salt, black pepper, water, nonstick cooking spray, and small amounts of oil, butter, flour and sugar, are not included in the count of ingredients. These ingredients are ones you always have on hand. In addition, optional ingredients and garnishes are not counted.

## ALMOST HOMEMADE

Some of the recipes in this book utilize convenience products, many from the American brands you know and love. You'll find products like soup mixes and seasoning mixes for a quick burst of flavor, pasta sauces that you can personalize with the addition of a few ingredients, flavored canned tomatoes to save a step, flavored cheese spreads that are halfway to an easy dip, and sweetened condensed milk for the beginning of a spur-of-the-moment dessert sauce. Cooking with convenience foods brings you the satisfaction of preparing comfort foods for your family, but without the bother of made-from-scratch recipes.

# CUTTING KITCHEN TIME

You don't have to renovate to make your kitchen more efficient. Little things like storing pot holders and dish towels in easily accessible places can make big differences. Eliminating items you rarely use can free up counter and storage space, too. Keep cooking tools like wooden spoons, spatulas and tongs in a utensil holder next to the range and you won't waste time rummaging through drawers for them. Store your favorite pots and pans towards the front of the cabinet or on an overhead rack. Basic spices should be readily available.

Post a shopping list within easy reach and add items to the list as you see they are running low. In fact, everyone in the family can add to the list. Try to minimize the number of dishes and utensils you use. Shred cheese or grate citrus peel on a plate that you can later pop into the dishwasher. Or, use disposable waxed paper or plastic wrap. Beat eggs for meat loaf or meatballs in a large bowl, then add the remaining ingredients; there's no need to use two bowls. Mix salad dressing ingredients in a bowl, then add the remaining salad items and toss.

Clean up as you go. Rinse dirty dishes and utensils and load them into the dishwasher as you prepare the meal. This will make cleanup a breeze. Consider plating food rather than serving it family style—there will be fewer dishes to wash.

# THE COOK'S PANTRY

Having a well-stocked pantry can make last-minute meals a cinch. You don't need a lot of space; as little as one shelf in a cabinet will store items, like spices and herbs, bouillon granules, pasta, canned tomatoes, flour, sugar, condensed soups, as well as extras of your favorite condiments. Customize your pantry to match your family's tastes and your cooking style. Gather your best-loved recipes and some new favorites from this cookbook; keep a supply of the shelf-stable and frozen ingredients needed to prepare them in your pantry. Last-minute trips to the grocery store will be a thing of the past.

So get started now and let this fabulous collection of easy recipes bring the joys of comfort foods to your twenty-first century family. Prepare and serve delicious meals that your family and friends will love without spending a lot of time in the kitchen. What could be a better gift for those you love?

# Quick Appetizers

## Quick Tip

Puff pastry dough cuts best with a sharp knife with a straight blade, such as a French chef's knife. Cut straight down rather than pulling the knife through the dough.

## SPINACH CHEESE BUNDLES

**1 container (6½ ounces) garlic- and herb-flavored spreadable cheese**
**½ cup chopped fresh spinach**
**1 package (17¼ ounces) frozen puff pastry, thawed**
**Sweet and sour or favorite dipping sauce (optional)**

1. Preheat oven to 400°F. Combine cheese, spinach and ¼ teaspoon black pepper in small bowl; mix well.

2. Roll out one sheet puff pastry dough on floured surface into 12-inch square. Cut into 16 (3-inch) squares. Place about 1 teaspoon cheese mixture in center of each square. Brush edges of squares with water. Bring edges together up over filling and twist tightly to seal; fan out corners of puff pastry.

3. Place bundles 2 inches apart on ungreased baking sheet. Bake about 13 minutes or until golden brown. Repeat with remaining sheet of puff pastry and cheese mixture. Serve warm with dipping sauce, if desired. *Makes 32 bundles*

## BACON–WRAPPED BREADSTICKS

**8 slices bacon**
**16 garlic-flavored breadsticks (about 8 inches long)**
**¾ cup grated Parmesan cheese**
**2 tablespoons chopped fresh parsley (optional)**

Cut bacon slices in half lengthwise. Wrap half slice of bacon diagonally around each breadstick. Combine Parmesan cheese and parsley, if desired, in shallow dish; set aside.

Place 4 breadsticks on double layer of paper towels in microwave oven. Microwave at HIGH 2 to 3 minutes or until bacon is cooked through. Immediately roll breadsticks in Parmesan mixture to coat. Repeat with remaining breadsticks.                                    *Makes 16 breadsticks*

## CHICKEN NACHOS

**22 (about 1 ounce) GUILTLESS GOURMET® Baked Tortilla Chips (yellow, red or blue corn)**
**½ cup (4 ounces) cooked and shredded boneless chicken breast**
**¼ cup chopped green onions**
**¼ cup (1 ounce) shredded Cheddar cheese**
**Sliced green and red chilies (optional)**

**Microwave Directions**
Spread tortilla chips on flat microwave-safe plate. Sprinkle chicken, onions and cheese over chips. Microwave on HIGH 30 seconds until cheese starts to bubble. Serve hot. Garnish with chilies, if desired.

**Conventional Directions**
Preheat oven to 325°F. Spread tortilla chips on baking sheet. Sprinkle chicken, onions and cheese over chips. Bake about 5 minutes or until cheese starts to bubble. Serve hot.

*Makes 22 nachos*

# PEPPER CHEESE COCKTAIL PUFFS

**½ package (17¼ ounces) frozen puff pastry, thawed**
**1 tablespoon Dijon mustard**
**½ cup (2 ounces) finely shredded Cheddar cheese**
**1 teaspoon cracked black pepper**
**1 egg**

1. Preheat oven to 400°F. Grease baking sheet.

2. Roll out 1 sheet puff pastry dough on well-floured surface to 14×10-inch rectangle. Spread half of dough (from 10-inch side) with mustard. Sprinkle with cheese and pepper. Fold dough over filling; roll gently to seal edges.

3. Cut lengthwise into 3 strips; cut each strip diagonally into 1½-inch pieces. Place on prepared baking sheets. Beat egg and 1 tablespoon water in small bowl; brush on appetizers.

4. Bake appetizers 12 to 15 minutes or until puffed and deep golden brown. Remove from baking sheet to wire rack to cool.                    *Makes about 20 appetizers*

**Prep and Bake Time:** 30 minutes

# PIGGY WRAPS

**1 package HILLSHIRE FARM® Lit'l Smokies**
**2 cans (8 ounces each) refrigerated crescent roll dough,**
**    cut into small triangles**

Preheat oven to 400°F.

Wrap individual Lit'l Smokies in dough triangles. Bake 5 minutes or until golden brown.

*Makes about 50 hors d'oeuvres*

TIP: Piggy Wraps may be frozen. To reheat in microwave, microwave at HIGH 1½ minutes or at MEDIUM-HIGH (70% power) 2 minutes. When reheated in microwave, dough will not be crisp.

## Quick Tip

Work quickly and efficiently when using puff pastry. The colder puff pastry is, the better it will puff in the hot oven. Also, this recipe for Pepper Cheese Cocktail Puffs can be easily doubled.

# LIPTON® ROASTED RED PEPPER & ONION DIP

**1 envelope LIPTON® RECIPE SECRETS® Onion Soup Mix***
**1 container (16 ounces) regular or light sour cream**
**1 jar (7 ounces) roasted red peppers, drained and
    chopped**

**Also terrific with LIPTON® RECIPE SECRETS® Savory Herb with Garlic
Soup Mix.*

1. In small bowl, combine all ingredients; chill at least
2 hours.

2. Serve with your favorite dippers.          *Makes 2 cups dip*

# PIZZA CRESCENTS

**1½ cups (6 ounces) shredded JARLSBERG LITE™ cheese**
**1 (6½-ounce) bag dry pizza crust mix**
**½ cup water**
  **All-purpose flour for dusting fingers**

Toss together cheese and pizza crust mix. Stir in water until
moistened, adding a few drops water, if necessary. Divide
dough into 6 parts, about ¼ cup each. Preheat oven to 425°F.

With clean, floured fingers, pat each dough piece into 6-inch
circle. Fill each with pizza sauce and/or assorted fillings
(suggestions follow). Fold dough over filling to create
semi-circle, pressing edges together. Place on nonstick or
greased pan; bake 15 minutes or until crisp and golden.

*Makes 6 servings*

TIP: Decorate with a few additional strands of shredded
Jarlsberg cheese, if desired, before baking.

FILLINGS: Fill each circle with 2 tablespoons pizza sauce
and 1 tablespoon shredded JARLSBERG LITE™ cheese; **or**
1 tablespoon applesauce or drained canned fruit cocktail,
dash of cinnamon or ground cloves, 1 tablespoon raisins or
chopped dried fruit; **or** 2 tablespoons ½-inch-dice firm tofu,
2 tablespoons chopped green onions, leftover cooked
vegetables (such as string beans, broccoli, corn) and
¼ teaspoon light soy sauce.

---

## Express Recipe

Beat 8 ounces of
cream cheese
with ⅓ cup prepared
pesto until well
blended. Serve this as
a spread with
crackers.

# SHRIMP AND SNOW PEA APPETIZERS WITH CURRANT MUSTARD SAUCE

**6 ounces fresh snow peas (about 36)**
**1½ pounds medium shrimp, cooked and peeled**

**Currant Mustard Sauce**
**¾ cup SMUCKER'S® Currant Jelly**
**¼ cup Dijon mustard**

Blanch snow peas in boiling salted water for 45 seconds. Immediately drain and rinse under cold water.

Wrap 1 blanched pea pod around each shrimp and secure with toothpick.

Combine jelly and mustard; beat with a fork or wire whisk until smooth. (Jelly will dissolve in about 5 minutes.) Serve sauce with appetizers.          *Makes 36 appetizers*

# CROSTINI

**¼ loaf whole wheat baguette (4 ounces)**
**4 plum tomatoes**
**1 cup (4 ounces) shredded part-skim mozzarella cheese**
**3 tablespoons prepared pesto sauce**

1. Preheat oven to 400°F. Slice baguette into 16 very thin, diagonal slices. Slice each tomato vertically into four ¼-inch slices.

2. Place baguette slices on nonstick baking sheet. Top each with 1 tablespoon cheese, then 1 slice tomato. Bake about 8 minutes or until bread is lightly toasted and cheese is melted. Remove from oven; top each crostini with about ½ teaspoon pesto sauce. Garnish with fresh basil, if desired. Serve warm.          *Makes 8 appetizer servings*

## Quick Tip

Blanching the snow peas for this recipe enhances their color and softens them so they can be easily wrapped around the shrimp. Plunging them in cold water stops the cooking process and cools them for easier handling.

## Quick Tip

Pesto is an uncooked sauce made with fresh basil leaves, garlic, pine nuts, Parmesan cheese and olive oil. A small amount of pesto adds intense flavor to breads, soups, pasta dishes and salad dressings.

# FAST PESTO FOCACCIA

**1 can (10 ounces) refrigerated pizza crust dough**
**2 tablespoons prepared pesto**
**4 sun-dried tomatoes packed in oil, drained**

1. Preheat oven to 425°F. Lightly grease 8×8×2-inch pan. Unroll pizza dough; fold in half and pat into pan.

2. Spread pesto evenly over dough. Chop tomatoes or snip with kitchen scissors; sprinkle over pesto. Press tomatoes into dough. Make indentations in dough every 2 inches using wooden spoon handle.

3. Bake 10 to 12 minutes or until golden brown. Cut into squares and serve warm or at room temperature.

*Makes 16 squares*

**Prep and Cook Time: 20 minutes**

# FRENCH ONION DIP

**1 container (16 ounces) sour cream**
**½ cup HELLMANN'S® or BEST FOODS® Real Mayonnaise**
**1 package KNORR® Recipe Classics™ French Onion Soup, Dip and Recipe Mix**

1. In medium bowl, combine all ingredients; chill.

2. Stir before serving. Serve with your favorite dippers.

*Makes about 2½ cups*

# BBQ RANCH DIP

**½ cup nonfat ranch dressing**
**3 tablespoons HUNT'S® Original Barbecue Sauce**

Combine ingredients; cover and chill.

*Makes 7 servings (2 tablespoons per serving)*

## HIDDEN VALLEY® SALSA RANCH DIP

**1 container (16 ounces) sour cream (2 cups)**
**1 packet (1 ounce) HIDDEN VALLEY® The Original Ranch®**
    **Dips Mix**
**½ cup thick and chunky salsa**
    **Chopped tomatoes and diced green chiles (optional)**
    **Tortilla chips, for dipping**

Combine sour cream and dips mix. Stir in salsa. Add
tomatoes and chiles, if desired. Chill 1 hour. Serve with
tortilla chips.                              *Makes 2½ cups*

## ALOUETTE® ELÉGANTE WITH RED PEPPER COULIS

**1 small jar roasted red peppers, drained**
**1 teaspoon olive oil**
**1 (6-ounce) package ALOUETTE® Elégante, Roasted**
    **Garlic and Pesto**
    **Paprika**
    **Fresh chopped chives or parsley**

To make red pepper coulis, add roasted red peppers and olive
oil to food processor; purée until smooth. Pour coulis into
center of 8-inch rimmed salad plate (a plain white plate works
best). Position Alouette Elégante in center of coulis. Sprinkle
paprika and chopped chives around rim of plate. Serve with
your favorite crusty bread.             *Makes 6 to 8 servings*

## HIDDEN VALLEY® SEAFOOD DIP

**1 cup cooked shrimp or crabmeat, finely chopped**
**1 cup (½ pint) sour cream**
**1 packet (1 ounce) HIDDEN VALLEY® The Original Ranch®**
    **Salad Dressing & Seasoning Mix**
**¼ cup chili sauce**

In medium bowl, combine all ingredients; refrigerate at least
1 hour before serving. Serve with crackers or assorted
vegetables for dipping.                        *Makes about 2 cups*

## Express Recipe

For a quick and easy spicy southwestern dip, combine ranch dressing and 2 chopped canned chipotle chilies in adobo sauce.

# BAKED APRICOT BRIE

**1 round (8 ounces) Brie cheese**
**⅓ cup apricot preserves**
**2 tablespoons sliced almonds**
**Cracked pepper or other assorted crackers**

1. Preheat oven to 400°F. Place cheese in small baking pan; spread top of cheese with preserves and sprinkle with almonds.

2. Bake about 10 to 12 minutes or until cheese begins to melt and lose its shape. Serve hot with crackers. Refrigerate leftovers; reheat before serving.    *Makes 6 servings*

TIP: Brie is a soft-ripened, unpressed cheese made from cow's milk. It has a distinctive round shape, edible white rind and creamy yellow interior. Avoid Brie that has a chalky center (it is underripe) or a strong ammonia odor (it is overripe). The cheese should give slightly to pressure and have an evenly colored, barely moist rind.

**Cook Time: 12 minutes**

# ZESTY BRUSCHETTA

**1 envelope LIPTON® RECIPE SECRETS® Savory Herb with Garlic Soup Mix**
**6 tablespoons BERTOLLI® Olive Oil***
**1 loaf French or Italian bread (about 18 inches long), sliced lengthwise**
**2 tablespoons shredded or grated Parmesan cheese**

*\*Substitution: Use ½ cup margarine or butter, melted.*

Preheat oven to 350°F. Blend savory herb with garlic soup mix and oil. Brush onto bread, then sprinkle with cheese.

Bake 12 minutes or until golden. Slice, then serve.
   *Makes 1 loaf, about 18 pieces*

## CHEESE STRAWS

½ cup (1 stick) butter, softened
⅛ teaspoon salt
  Dash ground red pepper
1 pound sharp Cheddar cheese, shredded, at room temperature
2 cups self-rising flour

Heat oven to 350°F. In mixer bowl, beat butter, salt and pepper until creamy. Add cheese; mix well. Gradually add flour, mixing until dough begins to form a ball. Form dough into ball with hands. Fit cookie press with small star plate; fill with dough according to manufacturer's directions. Press dough onto cookie sheets in 3-inch-long strips (or desired shapes). Bake 12 minutes, just until lightly browned. Cool completely on wire rack. Store tightly covered.

*Makes about 10 dozen*

*Favorite recipe from Southeast United Dairy Industry Association, Inc.*

## SPICY CHEESE 'N' CHILI DIP

1 pound BOB EVANS® Special Seasonings Roll Sausage
1 pound pasteurized process cheese spread
1 (10-ounce) can diced tomatoes with green chiles, drained
1 (14- to 16-ounce) bag tortilla chips

Crumble and cook sausage in medium skillet until browned. Drain on paper towels. Combine cheese and tomatoes in medium saucepan; heat until cheese is melted. Stir in sausage. Serve in warm bowl with tortilla chips.

*Makes 10 to 12 servings*

## CHUTNEY CHEESE DIP

1 (8-ounce) package cream cheese, softened
1 (8-ounce) container plain yogurt
½ cup chopped PATAK'S® Major Grey Mango Chutney

In medium bowl, combine all ingredients. Cover and refrigerate until serving time. Serve with fruit and crackers.

*Makes 2½ cups dip*

## CHUNKY HAWAIIAN SPREAD

**1 package (3 ounces) light cream cheese, softened**
**½ cup fat free or light sour cream**
**1 can (8 ounces) DOLE® Crushed Pineapple, well-drained**
**¼ cup mango chutney***
**Low fat crackers**

*\*If there are large pieces of fruit in chutney, cut them into small pieces.*

• Beat cream cheese, sour cream, crushed pineapple and chutney in bowl until blended. Cover and chill 1 hour or overnight. Serve with crackers. Refrigerate any leftover spread in airtight container for up to one week.

*Makes 2½ cups*

## STICKY WINGS

**24 chicken wings (about 4 pounds)**
**¾ cup WISH-BONE® Italian Dressing***
**1 cup apricot or peach preserves**
**1 tablespoon hot pepper sauce (optional)****

*\*Also terrific with WISH-BONE® Robusto Italian or Just 2 Good! Dressing.*
*\*\*Use more or less to taste desired.*

Cut tips off chicken wings (save tips for soup). Cut chicken wings in half at joint.

For marinade, blend Italian dressing, preserves and hot pepper sauce. In large, shallow nonaluminum baking dish or plastic bag, pour ½ of the marinade over chicken wings; toss to coat. Cover, or close bag, and marinate in refrigerator, turning occasionally, 3 to 24 hours. Refrigerate remaining marinade.

Remove wings, discarding marinade. Grill or broil wings, turning once and brushing frequently with refrigerated marinade, until wings are thoroughly cooked.

*Makes 48 appetizers*

# BANDITO BUFFALO WINGS

**1 package (1.25 ounces) ORTEGA® Taco Seasoning Mix**
**12 (about 1 pound *total*) chicken wings**
  **ORTEGA® Salsa (any flavor)**

**PREHEAT** oven to 375°F. Lightly grease 13×9-inch baking pan.

**PLACE** seasoning mix in heavy-duty plastic or paper bag. Add 3 chicken wings; shake well to coat. Place wings in prepared pan. Repeat until all wings have been coated.

**BAKE** for 35 to 40 minutes or until no longer pink near bone. Serve with salsa for dipping.

*Makes 6 appetizer servings*

# CHUNKY CHILI DIP

**1 can (4 ounces) chopped green chilies**
**2 tablespoons chopped red onion**
**1 tablespoon chopped fresh cilantro**
**1 package (8 ounces) light cream cheese, softened**

Combine chilies, onion, cilantro and $\frac{1}{8}$ teaspoon salt in small bowl.

Spread cream cheese on medium serving plate. Top with green chili mixture. Serve with assorted crackers or tortilla chips.                    *Makes $1\frac{1}{3}$ cups (11 servings)*

**Prep Time:** 13 minutes

# SAUSAGE CHEESE PUFFS

**1 pound BOB EVANS® Original Recipe Roll Sausage**
**2½ cups (10 ounces) shredded sharp Cheddar cheese**
  **2 cups biscuit mix**
  **½ cup water**
  **1 teaspoon baking powder**

Preheat oven to 350°F. Combine ingredients in large bowl until blended. Shape into 1-inch balls. Place on lightly greased baking sheets. Bake about 25 minutes or until golden brown. Serve hot. Refrigerate leftovers.

*Makes about 60 appetizers*

# HOLIDAY APPETIZER PUFFS

**1 sheet frozen puff pastry, thawed (½ of 17¼-ounce package)**
**2 tablespoons olive or vegetable oil**
  **Toppings: grated Parmesan cheese, sesame seeds, poppy seeds, dried dill weed, dried basil leaves, paprika, drained capers, pimiento-stuffed green olive slices**

1. Preheat oven to 425°F. Roll pastry on lightly floured surface to 13-inch square. Cut into shapes with cookie cutters (simple-shaped cutters work best). Place on ungreased baking sheets.

2. Brush cut-outs lightly with oil. Decorate with desired toppings.

3. Bake 6 to 8 minutes or until golden. Serve warm or at room temperature.          *Makes about 1½ dozen appetizers*

# FIESTA QUESO DIP

**1 can (14½ ounces) DEL MONTE® Diced Tomatoes with Garlic & Onion**
**1 pound jalapeño processed cheese, diced**
**¼ cup sliced green onions**
  **Tortilla chips**

1. Combine undrained tomatoes, cheese and green onions in medium saucepan.

2. Cook over low heat about 12 minutes or until cheese melts, stirring frequently. Serve hot with chips.
          *Makes 3½ cups*

**Prep Time:** 3 minutes
**Cook Time:** 12 minutes

---

## Express Recipe

For an elegant appetizer, pipe spreadable garlic or pesto-flavored cheese onto Belgian endive leaves and garnish with red bell pepper triangles or a sprig of parsley.

## ROASTED RED PEPPER SPREAD

**1 cup roasted red peppers, rinsed and drained**
**1 package (8 ounces) cream cheese, softened**
**1 packet (1 ounce) HIDDEN VALLEY® The Original Ranch®**
    **Salad Dressing & Seasoning Mix**
**Baguette slices and sliced ripe olives (optional)**

Blot dry red peppers. In a food processor fitted with a metal blade, combine peppers, cream cheese and salad dressing & seasoning mix; process until smooth. Spread on baguette slices and garnish with olives, if desired.     *Makes 2 cups*

## HIDDEN VALLEY® CHEESE FINGERS

**2 small loaves (8 ounces each) French bread, cut in half**
    **lengthwise**
**1 package (8 ounces) cream cheese, softened**
**1 packet (1 ounce) HIDDEN VALLEY® The Original Ranch®**
    **Salad Dressing & Seasoning Mix**
**4 cups assorted toppings, such as chopped onions, bell**
    **peppers and shredded cheese**

Slice bread crosswise into 1-inch fingers, leaving fingers attached to crust. Mix together cream cheese and salad dressing & seasoning mix. Spread on cut sides of bread. Sprinkle on desired toppings. Broil about 3 minutes or until brown and bubbly.     *Makes about 48 fingers*

## ORIGINAL RANCH® MEATBALLS

**1 pound ground beef**
**1 packet (1 ounce) HIDDEN VALLEY® The Original Ranch®**
    **Salad Dressing & Seasoning Mix**
**2 tablespoons butter or margarine**
**½ cup beef broth**

Combine ground beef and salad dressing & seasoning mix. Shape into meatballs. Melt butter in a skillet; brown meatballs on all sides. Add broth; cover and simmer 10 to 15 minutes or until cooked through. Serve warm with toothpicks.     *Makes 2 dozen meatballs*

## MEXICAN ROLL-UPS

**6 uncooked lasagna noodles**
**¾ cup prepared guacamole**
**¾ cup chunky salsa**
**¾ cup (3 ounces) shredded fat-free Cheddar cheese**

1. Cook lasagna noodles according to package directions, omitting salt. Rinse with cool water; drain. Cool.

2. Spread 2 tablespoons guacamole onto each noodle; top each with 2 tablespoons salsa and 2 tablespoons cheese.

3. Roll up noodles jelly-roll fashion. Cut each roll-up in half to form two equal-size roll-ups. Serve immediately with additional salsa, if desired, or cover with plastic wrap and refrigerate up to 3 hours.          *Makes 12 appetizers*

## HONEY NUT BRIE

**¼ cup honey**
**¼ cup coarsely chopped pecans**
**1 tablespoon brandy (optional)**
**1 wheel (14 ounces) Brie cheese (about 5-inch diameter)**

Combine honey, pecans and brandy, if desired, in small bowl. Place cheese on large round ovenproof platter or in 9-inch pie plate.

Bake in preheated 500°F oven 4 to 5 minutes or until cheese softens. Drizzle honey mixture over top of cheese. Bake 2 to 3 minutes longer or until topping is thoroughly heated. *Do not melt cheese.*          *Makes 16 to 20 servings*

TIP: Serve as party dish with crackers, tart apple wedges and seedless grapes.

# Quick Tip

Bacon cooks quickly with little mess in a microwave oven. Simply place slices, without overlapping, in a single layer between sheets of paper toweling. Microwave at HIGH about 1 minute per slice. Cool bacon before crumbling.

## CHEDDAR TOMATO BACON TOASTS

**1 jar (1 pound) RAGÚ® Cheese Creations!® Double Cheddar Sauce**
**1 medium tomato, chopped**
**5 slices bacon, crisp-cooked and crumbled (about ⅓ cup)**
**2 loaves Italian bread (each about 16 inches long), each cut into 16 slices**

1. Preheat oven to 350°F. In medium bowl, combine Ragú Cheese Creations! Sauce, tomato and bacon.

2. On baking sheet, arrange bread slices. Evenly top with sauce mixture.

3. Bake 10 minutes or until sauce mixture is bubbling. Serve immediately.                           *Makes 16 servings*

**Prep Time:** 10 minutes
**Cook Time:** 10 minutes

## ORIGINAL RANCH® DRUMMETTES

**1 packet (1 ounce) HIDDEN VALLEY® The Original Ranch® Salad Dressing & Seasoning Mix**
**¼ cup vegetable oil**
**24 chicken drummettes (about 2 pounds)**

Combine dressing mix and oil in large bowl. Add drummettes; toss well to coat. Arrange on rack placed in foil-lined baking pan; bake at 425°F for 25 minutes. Turn drummettes over; bake additional 20 minutes.
*Makes 24 drummettes*

SPICY HOT VARIATION: Add 2 tablespoons hot red pepper sauce to dressing mixture before coating.

SERVING SUGGESTION: Dip cooked drummettes in prepared Hidden Valley® Original Ranch® salad dressing.

# THE FAMOUS LIPTON® CALIFORNIA DIP

**1 envelope LIPTON® RECIPE SECRETS® Onion Soup Mix**
**1 container (16 ounces) regular or light sour cream**

1. In medium bowl, blend all ingredients; chill at least 2 hours.

2. Serve with your favorite dippers.

*Makes about 2 cups dip*

TIP: For a creamier dip, add more sour cream.

SENSATIONAL SPINACH DIP: Add 1 package (10 ounces) frozen chopped spinach, thawed and squeezed dry.

CALIFORNIA SEAFOOD DIP: Add 1 cup finely chopped cooked clams, crabmeat or shrimp, ¼ cup chili sauce and 1 tablespoon horseradish.

CALIFORNIA BACON DIP: Add ⅓ cup crumbled cooked bacon or bacon bits.

CALIFORNIA BLUE CHEESE DIP: Add ¼ pound crumbled blue cheese and ¼ cup finely chopped walnuts.

# FAST GUACAMOLE AND "CHIPS"

**2 ripe avocados**
**½ cup restaurant-style chunky salsa**
**¼ teaspoon hot pepper sauce (optional)**
**½ seedless cucumber, sliced into ⅛-inch rounds**

1. Cut avocados in half; remove and discard pits. Scoop flesh into medium bowl. Mash with fork.

2. Add salsa and pepper sauce, if desired; mix well.

3. Transfer guacamole to serving bowl; surround with cucumber "chips".          *Makes 8 servings, about 1¾ cups*

## Express Recipe

Place an 8-ounce brick of softened cream cheese on a serving plate. Stir 3 to 4 tablespoons of hot pepper jelly in a small bowl until it is spreadable. Spread the jelly over the cream cheese. Serve this easy appetizer with crackers and tortilla chips.

# FESTIVE FRANKS

**1 can (8 ounces) crescent roll dough**
**5½ teaspoons barbecue sauce**
**⅓ cup finely shredded sharp Cheddar cheese**
**8 hot dogs**
**¼ teaspoon poppy seeds (optional)**

1. Preheat oven to 350°F. Spray large baking sheet with nonstick cooking spray; set aside.

2. Unroll dough and separate into 8 triangles. Cut each triangle in half lengthwise to make 2 triangles. Lightly spread barbecue sauce over each triangle. Sprinkle with cheese.

3. Cut each hot dog in half; trim off rounded ends. Place one hot dog piece at large end of one dough triangle. Roll up jelly-roll style from wide end. Place point side down on prepared baking sheet. Sprinkle with poppy seeds, if desired. Repeat with remaining hot dog pieces and dough.

4. Bake 13 minutes or until dough is golden brown. Cool 1 to 2 minutes on baking sheet. Serve with additional barbecue sauce for dipping, if desired.     *Makes 16 servings*

# GREEN ONION DIP

**1 packet (1 ounce) HIDDEN VALLEY® The Original Ranch® Salad Dressing & Seasoning Mix**
**1 cup mayonnaise**
**1 cup (½ pint) sour cream**
**½ cup finely chopped green onions**

In medium bowl, whisk together all ingredients. Refrigerate at least 1 hour before serving. Serve with fresh vegetables, such as cauliflowerets, carrot and celery sticks, cucumber slices, tomato wedges or turnip chips.

*Makes about 2½ cups*

# SOUTHWESTERN CHILI CHEESE EMPANADAS

**¾ cup (3 ounces) finely shredded taco-flavored cheese***
**⅓ cup diced green chilies, drained**
**1 package (15 ounces) refrigerated pie crusts**
**1 egg**

*\*If taco-flavored cheese is unavailable, toss ¾ cup shredded marbled Monterey Jack cheese with ½ teaspoon chili powder.*

1. Combine cheese and chilies in small bowl.

2. Unfold 1 pastry crust on floured surface. Roll into 13-inch circle. Cut dough into 16 rounds using 3-inch cookie cutter, rerolling scraps as necessary. Repeat with remaining crust to total 32 circles.

3. Spoon 1 teaspoon cheese mixture in center of each dough round. Fold round in half, sealing edge with tines of fork.

4. Place empanadas on wax paper-lined baking sheets; freeze, uncovered, 1 hour or until firm. Place in resealable plastic food storage bags. Freeze up to 2 months.

5. To complete recipe, preheat oven to 400°F. Place frozen empanadas on ungreased baking sheet. Beat egg and 1 tablespoon water in small bowl; brush on empanadas. Sprinkle with chili powder, if desired.

6. Bake 12 to 17 minutes or until golden brown. Remove from baking sheet to wire rack to cool.          *Makes 32 appetizers*

SERVING SUGGESTION: Serve empanadas with salsa and sour cream.

# MAPLE DIJON DIP

**1 cup HIDDEN VALLEY® The Original Ranch® Dressing**
**4 teaspoons pure maple syrup**
**1 teaspoon Dijon mustard**
**Hot cooked chicken nuggets (optional)**

Stir together dressing, syrup and mustard in a small bowl. Chill 30 minutes. Serve with chicken nuggets, if desired.

*Makes 1 cup*

## BACON CHEESE SPREAD

**½ cup FLEISCHMANN'S® Original Margarine, softened**
**¼ cup grated Parmesan cheese**
**¼ cup real bacon bits**
**¼ cup minced onion**

1. Blend margarine, cheese, bacon and onion in small bowl with mixer at medium speed. Cover and store in refrigerator.

2. Serve as a topping for baked potatoes or as a spread for toasted Italian bread.                    *Makes about 1 cup*

**Prep Time:** 10 minutes
**Total Time:** 10 minutes

## MARINATE WHILE YOU BAKE DRUMMETTES

**3 pounds chicken drummettes**
**1 bottle (12 ounces) LAWRY'S® Teriyaki Marinade with Pineapple Juice, divided**

Preheat oven to 450°F. Spray 15×10×1-inch jelly-roll pan with nonstick cooking spray. Place chicken in pan; pour 1 cup Teriyaki Marinade over chicken. Bake 40 to 45 minutes or until browned, basting with additional Marinade every 10 minutes and turning chicken over halfway through baking time.

*Makes appetizers for 12 to 15 or*
*several meals for 'little' eaters*

**Prep Time:** 4 minutes
**Cook Time:** 40 to 45 minutes

## RED PEPPER DIP

**6 ounces roasted red peppers, rinsed and drained**
**1 cup HIDDEN VALLEY® The Original Ranch® Dressing**
**1 package (8 ounces) cream cheese, softened**
**Hot cooked chicken nuggets**

In a food processor fitted with a metal blade, purée peppers. Add dressing and cream cheese; process until smooth. Chill 30 minutes. Serve with chicken nuggets.          *Makes 2 cups*

## SAUSAGE PINWHEELS

**2 cups biscuit mix**
**½ cup milk**
**¼ cup butter or margarine, melted**
**1 pound BOB EVANS® Original Recipe Roll Sausage**

Combine biscuit mix, milk and butter in large bowl until blended. Refrigerate 30 minutes. Divide dough into two portions. Roll out one portion on floured surface to ⅛-inch-thick rectangle, about 10×7 inches. Spread with half the sausage. Roll lengthwise into long roll. Repeat with remaining dough and sausage. Place rolls in freezer until firm enough to cut easily. Preheat oven to 400°F. Cut rolls into thin slices. Place on baking sheets. Bake 15 minutes or until golden brown. Serve hot. Refrigerate leftovers.

*Makes 48 pinwheels*

NOTE: This recipe may be doubled. Refreeze after slicing. When ready to serve, thaw slices in refrigerator and bake.

## MANWICH WINGS

**2 pounds chicken wing drummettes**
**1 can (15.5 ounces) HUNT'S® Manwich Original Sloppy**
    **Joe Sauce**
**¼ cup Dijon mustard**
**¼ cup honey**
**½ teaspoon salt**

In large bowl, combine all ingredients; mix well. Marinate 1 hour or overnight.

Remove drummettes from marinade, reserving marinade. On large baking sheet lined with foil, arrange drummettes in single layer. Bake at 350°F 30 minutes. Drain baking sheet. Turn drummettes over; pour reserved marinade over wings. Bake at 350°F 30 minutes, basting occasionally.

*Makes about 2 dozen wings*

# Easy Meat Dishes

## GRILLED SHERRY PORK CHOPS

**¼ cup HOLLAND HOUSE® Sherry Cooking Wine**
**¼ cup GRANDMA'S® Molasses**
**2 tablespoons soy sauce**
**4 pork chops (1 inch thick)**

In plastic bowl, combine sherry, molasses and soy sauce; pour over pork chops. Cover; refrigerate 30 minutes. Prepare grill. Drain pork chops; reserve marinade. Grill pork chops over medium-high heat 20 to 30 minutes or until pork is no longer pink in center, turning once and brushing frequently with reserved marinade.* Discard any remaining marinade.

*Makes 4 servings*

*Do not baste during last 5 minutes of grilling.*

## HAM SCRAMBLE

**2 tablespoons vegetable oil or butter**
**1 pound HILLSHIRE FARM® Ham, cut into bite-size pieces**
**2 onions, thinly sliced**
**2 apples, cored and sliced**

Heat oil in large skillet over medium-high heat. Sauté Ham, onions and apples until onions and apples are tender, stirring constantly.

*Makes 4 to 6 servings*

# ROAST LEG OF LAMB

**3 tablespoons coarse-grained mustard**
**2 cloves garlic, minced**
**1½ teaspoons dried rosemary, crushed**
**1 leg of lamb, well trimmed, boned, rolled and tied**
   **(about 4 pounds)**
**Mint jelly (optional)**

Preheat oven to 400°F. Combine mustard, garlic, rosemary and ½ teaspoon black pepper. Rub mustard mixture over lamb.* Place roast on meat rack in foil-lined, shallow roasting pan. Roast 15 minutes. *Reduce oven temperature to 325°F;* roast about 20 minutes per pound for medium or until internal temperature reaches 145°F when tested with meat thermometer inserted into thickest part of roast.

Transfer roast to cutting board; cover with foil. Let stand 10 to 15 minutes before carving. Internal temperature will continue to rise 5° to 10°F during stand time.

Cut strings; discard. Carve roast into thin slices; serve with mint jelly, if desired.          *Makes 10 to 12 servings*

*At this point lamb may be covered and refrigerated up to 24 hours before roasting.*

# MANWICH MEATLOAF

**1 can (15.5 ounces) HUNT'S® Manwich Original Sloppy**
   **Joe Sauce, divided**
**1 pound ground beef**
**¾ cup quick-cooking oats**
**2 eggs**

In large bowl, combine ½ can Manwich Sauce, ground beef, oats and eggs; mix well. Press into loaf pan. Bake at 350°F for 30 minutes; drain off drippings from pan.

Pour remaining ½ can Manwich Sauce evenly over meatloaf. Bake at 350°F 30 minutes.          *Makes 4 to 6 servings*

## Quick Tip

For a more intense garlic flavor inside the leg of lamb, cut garlic into slivers. Cut small pockets at random intervals throughout the roast with the tip of a sharp knife; insert the garlic slivers.

## MAPLE–MUSTARD PORK CHOPS

**2 tablespoons maple syrup, divided**
**1 tablespoon olive oil**
**2 teaspoons whole-grain mustard**
**2 center-cut pork loin chops (6 ounces each)**

1. Preheat oven to 375°F. Combine maple syrup, olive oil and mustard in small bowl. Brush syrup mixture over both sides of pork chops.

2. Spray medium ovenproof skillet with nonstick cooking spray; heat over medium-high heat. Add chops; brown on both sides. Add ⅓ cup water; cover and bake 20 to 30 minutes or until barely pink in center.

*Makes 2 servings*

## FIRECRACKER BARBECUE PORK

**1 boneless pork loin roast, about 2 pounds**
**¾ cup barbecue sauce**
**⅓ cup orange marmalade**
**½ teaspoon hot pepper sauce**
**1 teaspoon grated horseradish (optional)**

Season roast with salt and pepper; place over indirect heat on medium-hot grill. Stir together remaining ingredients and baste roast every 8 to 10 minutes with mixture, until roast is done (internal temperature measured with meat thermometer 155° to 160°F), about 30 to 45 minutes. Let roast rest for 5 to 8 minutes before slicing to serve. Discard any leftover basting mixture.

*Makes 4 to 6 servings*

*Favorite recipe from **National Pork Board***

# Quick Tip

A cast iron skillet is a good choice for preparing Maple-Mustard Pork Chops. It will brown the chops slowly and evenly, then it can be transferred to the oven for baking.

# CARAMELIZED BACON

**12 slices (12 ounces) thick-sliced bacon, preferably apple
    wood smoked
½ cup packed light brown sugar
 2 tablespoons water
½ teaspoon ground red pepper**

1. Preheat oven to 375°F. Line 15×10-inch jelly-roll pan with heavy-duty foil. Spray wire rack with nonstick cooking spray; place in prepared pan.

2. Cut bacon in half crosswise; arrange in single layer on prepared wire rack.

3. Combine sugar, water and red pepper in small bowl; mix well. Brush generously over surface of bacon.

4. Bake bacon 20 to 25 minutes or until bacon is very brown, but not burned. Immediately transfer to serving platter; cool completely.      *Makes 6 servings*

NOTE: Bacon may be prepared up to 3 days ahead, stored between sheets of waxed paper in resealable plastic food storage bag and refrigerated. Let stand at room temperature at least 30 minutes before serving.

# GARLIC–PEPPER STEAK

**1¼ teaspoons LAWRY'S® Garlic Powder With Parsley
  1 pound sirloin steak
1¼ teaspoons LAWRY'S® Seasoned Pepper
½ teaspoon LAWRY'S® Seasoned Salt**

Press Garlic Powder With Parsley into both sides of steak with back of spoon. Sprinkle both sides with Seasoned Pepper and Seasoned Salt. Cover and refrigerate for 30 minutes; grill or broil for about 4 to 7 minutes per side or until desired doneness.      *Makes 4 servings*

SERVING SUGGESTION: Serve with hot baked potatoes and a crisp green salad.

**Prep Time:** 3 to 4 minutes
**Cook Time:** 8 to 14 minutes

**Quick Tip**

When you're in a hurry, you can save time in the kitchen by choosing ready-to-use chopped lettuce and packaged croutons.

## BEEF CAESAR SALAD

**1 bag (10 ounces) ready-to-use chopped romaine lettuce**
**2 tablespoons Caesar salad dressing**
**1 boneless beef top sirloin steak (about 1 pound)**
**2 slices whole wheat bread, toasted and cut into**
  **32 croutons**

1. Toss lettuce with dressing in large salad bowl. Divide salad greens evenly among 4 plates.

2. Cut steak lengthwise in half, then crosswise into ⅛-inch-thick strips. Sprinkle with black pepper. Spray 12-inch nonstick skillet with vegetable cooking spray and heat over high heat. Add beef; stir-fry 2 minutes or until beef is barely pink in center.

3. Top lettuce mixture with ¼ of steak strips. Season with pepper and top with 8 croutons.        *Makes 4 servings*

SERVING SUGGESTION: Serve with tomato soup or a meatless vegetable soup such as minestrone.

## CREAMY BEEF AND VEGETABLE CASSEROLE

**1 pound lean ground beef**
**1 small onion, chopped**
**1 bag (16 ounces) BIRDS EYE® frozen Farm Fresh**
  **Mixtures Broccoli, Corn & Red Peppers**
**1 can (10¾ ounces) cream of mushroom soup**

• In medium skillet, brown beef and onion; drain excess fat.

• Meanwhile, in large saucepan, cook vegetables according to package directions; drain.

• Stir in beef mixture and soup. Cook over medium heat until heated through.        *Makes 4 servings*

SERVING SUGGESTION: Serve over rice and sprinkle with ½ cup shredded Cheddar cheese.

**Prep Time:** 5 minutes
**Cook Time:** 10 to 15 minutes

# ORIENTAL BEEF KABOBS

**1 tablespoon olive oil**
**1 tablespoon soy sauce**
**1 tablespoon seasoned rice vinegar**
**4 purchased beef kabobs**

1. Preheat broiler. Position oven rack about 4 inches from heat source.

2. Whisk together oil, soy sauce and vinegar; brush on kabobs.

3. Arrange kabobs on rack of broiler pan. Broil 10 minutes or to desired doneness, turning after 5 minutes. Serve with Green Rice, if desired. *Makes 4 servings*

# SLOW COOKER TACO SHREDDED BEEF

**1 boneless beef chuck roast (4 to 4½ pounds)**
**2 packages (1.0 ounce each) LAWRY'S® Taco Spices & Seasonings**
**1 medium onion, halved and sliced**
**2 teaspoons LAWRY'S® Seasoned Salt**

**Slow Cooker Directions**
Trim and discard all fat from meat; place meat in slow cooker. Sprinkle both packages of Taco Spices & Seasonings over meat and top with onion. Cover and cook on LOW for 8 to 10 hours. Remove beef to platter and shred with fork. Return meat to juices in slow cooker; stir in Seasoned Salt. Serve shredded meat in tacos, burritos, taquitos, flautas, on rolls or over cooked rice.

*Makes 8 to 10 servings (or two meals serving 4 to 5)*

**Prep Time:** 10 minutes
**Slow Cooker Time:** 8 to 10 hours

## Express Recipe

To prepare Green Rice, bring 2 cups of chicken broth to a boil in a medium saucepan. Stir in 1 cup uncooked rice; reduce heat to low. Simmer, covered, for 14 minutes or until the rice is tender and all of the water is absorbed. Stir in ¼ cup *each* chopped green onions and minced parsley and 1 tablespoon butter.

## MARINATED PORK ROAST

**½ cup GRANDMA'S® Molasses**
**½ cup Dijon mustard**
**¼ cup tarragon vinegar**
**Boneless pork loin roast (3 to 4 pounds)**

1. In large plastic bowl, combine molasses, mustard and tarragon vinegar; mix well. Add pork to molasses mixture, turning to coat all sides. Marinate, covered, 1 to 2 hours at room temperature or overnight in refrigerator, turning several times.

2. Heat oven to 325°F. Remove pork from marinade; reserve marinade. Place pork in shallow roasting pan. Cook for 1 to 2 hours or until meat thermometer inserted into thickest part of roast reaches 160°F, basting with marinade* every 30 minutes; discard remaining marinade. Slice roast and garnish, if desired.                    *Makes 6 to 8 servings*

*\*Do not baste during last 5 minutes of cooking.*

## GRILLED SMOKED SAUSAGE

**1 cup apricot or pineapple preserves**
**1 tablespoon lemon juice**
**1½ pounds smoked sausage**

Heat preserves in small saucepan until melted. Strain; reserve fruit pieces. Combine strained preserve liquid with lemon juice in a small bowl to make glaze.

Oil hot grid to help prevent sticking. Grill whole sausage on an uncovered grill, over low KINGSFORD® Briquets, 10 minutes. Halfway through cooking, baste with glaze, then turn and continue grilling until heated through. Remove sausage from grill; baste with glaze. Garnish with fruit pieces.
                                          *Makes 4 to 5 servings*

## HICKORY SMOKED HAM WITH MAPLE-MUSTARD SAUCE

**Hickory chunks or chips for smoking**
**1 fully cooked boneless ham (about 5 pounds)**
**¾ cup maple syrup**
**¾ cup spicy brown mustard or Dijon mustard**

Soak about 4 wood chunks or several handfuls of wood chips in water; drain. If using a canned ham, scrape off any gelatin. If using another type of fully cooked ham, such as a bone-in shank, trim most of the fat, leaving a ⅛-inch layer. (The thinner the fat layer, the better the glaze will adhere to the ham.)

Arrange low KINGSFORD® Briquets on each side of a rectangular metal or foil drip pan. Pour in hot tap water to fill pan half full. Add soaked wood (all the chunks; part of the chips) to the fire.

Oil hot grid to help prevent sticking. Place ham on grid directly above drip pan. Grill ham, on a covered grill, 20 to 30 minutes per pound, until a meat thermometer inserted in the thickest part registers 140°F. If your grill has a thermometer, maintain a cooking temperature of about 200°F. For best flavor, cook slowly over low coals, adding a few briquets to both sides of the fire every hour, or as necessary, to maintain a constant temperature. Add more soaked hickory chips every 20 to 30 minutes.

Meanwhile, prepare Maple-Mustard Sauce by mixing maple syrup and mustard in small bowl; set aside most of the syrup mixture to serve as a sauce. Brush ham with remaining mixture several times during the last 45 minutes of cooking. Let ham stand 10 minutes before slicing. Slice and serve with Maple-Mustard Sauce.                *Makes 12 to 15 servings*

NOTE: Keep the briquet temperature low and replenish the hickory chips every 20 to 30 minutes.

*Quick Tip*

Most of the hams available today are fully cooked and need only to be heated to a temperature of 140°F. If you buy a partially cooked ham, often labeled "cook before eating," it needs to be cooked to 160°F.

## BRONZED PORK CHOPS

**1 tablespoon unsalted butter**
**6 (6-ounce) pork chops, about ¾ inch thick, at room**
**temperature (see Note)**
**1 tablespoon Chef Paul Prudhomme's Pork & Veal**
**Magic® or Chef Paul Prudhomme's Meat Magic®**

Melt the butter in pan or skillet large enough to hold pork chops; set aside.

Heat 10-inch skillet, preferably nonstick, over high heat to 350°F, about 4 minutes.

Dip chops in melted butter to coat both sides lightly and evenly. Place meat on plate and sprinkle (don't pour) ¼ teaspoon Pork and Veal (or Meat) Magic on one side of each chop. Carefully place chops, two at a time, seasoned side down, in 10-inch skillet and reduce heat to medium. Sprinkle ¼ teaspoon Pork and Veal (or Meat) Magic on top of each chop. Cook, turning several times, to desired doneness. Serve hot. Wipe out skillet; reheat to 350°F. Repeat process with remaining chops. Serve immediately.

*Makes 6 servings*

NOTE: If you must use cold meat, you will have to adjust the cooking time and turn the chops almost continuously to avoid burning.

## ORANGE MUSTARD PORK CHOP SKILLET

**4 top loin pork chops**
**⅓ cup orange juice**
**3 tablespoons soy sauce**
**2 tablespoons honey mustard**

In nonstick skillet, brown chops on one side over medium-high heat; turn chops; stir in remaining ingredients. Lower heat; simmer covered for 6 to 8 minutes.

*Makes 4 servings*

*Favorite recipe from* **National Pork Board**

---

### Express Recipe

Make an easy Asian marinade for pork by combining ⅓ cup reduced-sodium soy sauce, 3 tablespoons red wine vinegar, 2 tablespoons peanut oil and 1 tablespoon *each* minced garlic and fresh ginger.

## CORN DOGS

**8 hot dogs**
**8 wooden craft sticks**
**1 package (about 16 ounces) refrigerated grand-size**
    **corn biscuits**
**⅓ cup *French's*® Classic Yellow® Mustard**
**8 slices American cheese, cut in half**

1. Preheat oven to 350°F. Insert 1 wooden craft stick halfway into each hot dog; set aside.

2. Separate biscuits. On floured board, press or roll each biscuit into a 7×4-inch oval. Spread 2 *teaspoons* mustard lengthwise down center of each biscuit. Top each with 2 pieces of cheese. Place hot dog in center of biscuit. Fold top of dough over end of hot dog. Fold sides towards center enclosing hot dog. Pinch edges to seal.

3. Place corn dogs, seam-side down, on greased baking sheet. Bake 20 to 25 minutes or until golden brown. Cool slightly before serving.      *Makes 8 servings*

TIP: Corn dogs may be made without wooden craft sticks.

**Prep Time:** 15 minutes
**Cook Time:** 20 minutes

## CARIBBEAN ROAST PORK

**1 (3-pound) pork loin roast**
**2 teaspoons olive oil**
**1 tablespoon black pepper**
**1 teaspoon ground nutmeg**
**1 teaspoon ground cinnamon**

Blend oil, pepper, nutmeg and cinnamon in small bowl. Brush mixture evenly onto roast. Place pork in shallow pan; roast in 350°F oven for 1 to 1½ hours or until internal temperature is 155°F. Remove pork from oven; let stand 10 minutes before slicing.      *Makes 12 servings*

*Favorite recipe from **National Pork Board***

---

# Express Recipe

Take advantage of the quick-cooking convenience of pork tenderloin to make this easy dish for three or four. Cut 1 (12- to 16-ounce) pork tenderloin into ½-inch-thick slices. Sprinkle meat with a garlic pepper blend. Cook meat in a large skillet lightly sprayed with nonstick cooking spray. Cook the meat on medium heat until it is barely pink in the center. Remove meat from the skillet and add 3 tablespoons of brandy. Cook for 30 seconds, then whisk in 1½ tablespoons butter. Serve the sauce over the pork.

# PORK MEDALLIONS WITH MARSALA

**1 pound pork tenderloin, cut into ½-inch slices**
**2 tablespoons olive oil**
**1 clove garlic, minced**
**½ cup sweet marsala wine**

1. Lightly dust pork with flour. Heat oil in large skillet over medium-high heat until hot. Add pork slices; cook 3 minutes per side or until browned. Remove from pan. Reduce heat to medium.

2. Add garlic to skillet; cook and stir 1 minute. Add wine and pork; cook 3 minutes or until pork is barely pink in center. Remove pork from skillet. Stir in 2 tablespoons chopped parsley, if desired. Simmer wine mixture 2 to 3 minutes or until slightly thickened. Serve over pork.

*Makes 4 servings*

TIP: For a special touch, sprinkle with chopped red onion just before serving.

NOTE: Marsala is rich smoky-flavored wine imported from the Mediterranean island of Sicily. This sweet varietal is served with dessert or used for cooking. Dry Marsala is served as a before-dinner drink.

**Prep and Cook Time:** 20 minutes

# MAHOGANY CHOPS

**4 top loin pork chops**
**6 tablespoons teriyaki sauce**
**2 tablespoons molasses (or ketchup)**

Season chops with salt and pepper; grill over medium-hot coals, basting with teriyaki and molasses.

*Makes 4 servings*

*Favorite recipe from **National Pork Board***

# MARINATED FLANK STEAK WITH PINEAPPLE

**1 can (15¼ ounces) DEL MONTE® Sliced Pineapple In Its Own Juice**
**¼ cup teriyaki sauce**
**2 tablespoons honey**
**1 pound beef flank steak**

1. Drain pineapple, reserving 2 tablespoons juice. Set aside pineapple for later use.

2. Combine reserved juice, teriyaki sauce and honey in shallow 2-quart dish; mix well. Add meat; turn to coat. Cover and refrigerate at least 30 minutes or overnight.

3. Remove meat from marinade, reserving marinade. Grill meat over hot coals (or broil), brushing occasionally with reserved marinade. Cook about 4 minutes on each side for rare; about 5 minutes on each side for medium; or about 6 minutes on each side for well done. During last 4 minutes of cooking, grill pineapple until heated through.

4. Slice meat across grain; serve with pineapple. Garnish, if desired.    *Makes 4 servings*

NOTE: Marinade that has come into contact with raw meat must be discarded or boiled for several minutes before serving with cooked food.

**Prep and Marinate Time:** 35 minutes
**Cook Time:** 10 minutes

## Express Recipe

For a quick dinner, brown four thawed lean beef patties in a large skillet over medium heat. Add 1½ cups pasta sauce with onion and 2 small zucchini, cut into thin slices. Cover and cook 12 to 15 minutes or until beef is no longer pink in center. Sprinkle with 1 cup shredded mozzarella cheese. Remove the skillet from the heat and let it stand, covered, for 5 minutes or until the cheese melts. Serve with spaghetti, if desired.

## SMOTHERED MEXICAN PORK CHOPS

**1 tablespoon vegetable oil**
**4 boneless thin-cut pork chops (about ¾ pound)**
**1 can (14½ ounces) chunky tomatoes, salsa- or**
   **Cajun-style**
**1 can (16 ounces) black beans, drained**
**2 cups BIRDS EYE® frozen Farm Fresh Mixtures Broccoli,**
   **Corn and Red Peppers***

*\*Or, substitute 2 cups Birds Eye® frozen Corn.*

• Heat oil in large skillet over high heat. Add pork; cook until browned, about 4 minutes per side.

• Add tomatoes; reduce heat to medium. Cover and cook 5 minutes. Uncover and push pork to side of skillet.

• Add beans and vegetables. Place pork on top of vegetables. Increase heat to medium-high; cover and cook 5 minutes or until heated through.     *Makes about 4 servings*

**Prep Time:** 5 minutes
**Cook Time:** 20 minutes

## MUSTARD–CRUSTED PORK ROAST

**1 boneless pork loin roast, about 2 pounds**
**2 tablespoons spicy mustard**
**1 cup garlic croutons, crushed***

*\*Place croutons in plastic bag, roll with rolling pin until crushed.*

Heat oven to 400°F. Season roast with salt and pepper, place in shallow pan and roast for 30 minutes; remove from oven. Spread surface with mustard and sprinkle with crouton crumbs. Return to oven and continue to roast for 10 to 15 minutes longer, until meat thermometer registers 155°F.

*Makes 4 to 6 servings*

*Favorite recipe from* **National Pork Board**

---

## Express Recipe

If you're out of barbecue sauce, simply combine equal parts of steak sauce and ketchup. For a spicy version, season to taste with hot pepper sauce.

## FRAGRANT BEEF WITH GARLIC SAUCE

**1 boneless beef top sirloin steak (about 1¼ pounds)**
**⅓ cup reduced-sodium teriyaki sauce**
**10 large cloves garlic, peeled**
**½ cup fat-free reduced-sodium beef broth**

1. Place beef in large resealable plastic bag. Pour teriyaki sauce over beef. Seal bag; turn to coat. Marinate in refrigerator at least 30 minutes or up to 4 hours.

2. Combine garlic and broth in small saucepan. Bring to a boil over high heat. Reduce heat. Simmer, uncovered, 5 minutes. Cover and simmer 8 to 9 minutes until garlic is softened. Transfer to blender or food processor; process until smooth.

3. Meanwhile, drain beef; reserve marinade. Place beef on rack of broiler pan. Brush with half of reserved marinade. Broil 5 to 6 inches from heat 6 minutes. Turn beef; brush with remaining marinade. Broil 6 minutes for medium-rare doneness or until desired doneness.

4. Slice beef thinly; serve with garlic sauce and rice, if desired.
*Makes 4 servings*

## SALSA CHOPS

**4 pork chops, ¾ inch thick**
**Salt and pepper, to taste**
**1 teaspoon vegetable oil**
**1½ cups salsa**

Season chops with salt and pepper. Heat oil in large nonstick skillet over medium-high heat and brown chops on one side, about 3 to 4 minutes. Turn chops and add salsa to skillet. Bring to a boil; lower heat. Cover and simmer for 8 to 10 minutes.
*Makes 4 servings*

*Favorite recipe from **National Pork Board***

## Express Recipe

Make a paste with 3 cloves of minced garlic, 1 teaspoon of dried rosemary, 1 teaspoon coarse salt and ½ teaspoon of cracked black pepper. Use it as a rub on beef and lamb roasts.

## CRANBERRY–ONION PORK ROAST

**1 boneless pork loin roast (about 2 pounds)**
**1 (16-ounce) can whole cranberry sauce**
**1 package (1 ounce) dry onion soup mix**

Season roast with salt and pepper; place over indirect heat on grill; stir together cranberry sauce and onion soup mix and heat, covered, in microwave until hot (about 1 minute). Baste roast with cranberry mixture every 10 minutes until roast is done (internal temperature with a meat thermometer is 155° to 160°F), about 30 to 45 minutes; let roast rest about 5 to 8 minutes before slicing to serve. Heat any leftover basting mixture to boiling; stir and boil for 5 minutes. Serve alongside roast.                    *Makes 4 to 6 servings*

*Favorite recipe from* **National Pork Board**

## GRILLED SAUSAGE WITH APRICOT–MUSTARD GLAZE

**½ cup SMUCKER'S® Apricot Preserves**
**½ cup Dijon-style mustard**
**1 pound smoked pork sausage**
**4 French sandwich rolls**

Combine preserves and mustard; blend well. Set aside.

Cut pork sausage into 2-inch pieces and place on baking sheet. Grill or broil for 4 minutes; turn and cook for another 4 minutes.

Remove baking sheet from the heat and dip each piece in apricot-mustard glaze. Return to broiler or grill and cook for 2 more minutes or until lightly browned. Divide among sandwich rolls; serve with additional apricot-mustard glaze on the side.                    *Makes 4 servings*

# ROSEMARY–CRUSTED LEG OF LAMB

**¼ cup Dijon mustard**
**2 large cloves garlic, minced**
**1 boneless butterflied leg of lamb (sirloin half, about 2½ pounds), well trimmed**
**3 tablespoons chopped fresh rosemary *or* 1 tablespoon dried rosemary, crushed**
**Mint jelly (optional)**

1. Prepare grill for direct cooking.

2. Combine mustard and garlic in small bowl; spread half of mixture over one side of lamb. Sprinkle with half of chopped rosemary; pat into mustard mixture. Turn lamb over; repeat with remaining mustard mixture and rosemary. Insert meat thermometer into center of thickest part of lamb.

3. Place lamb on grid. Grill lamb, on covered grill, over medium coals 35 to 40 minutes or until thermometer registers 160°F for medium or until desired doneness is reached, turning every 10 minutes.

4. Transfer lamb to carving board; tent with foil. Let stand 10 minutes before carving into thin slices. Serve with mint jelly, if desired.

*Makes 8 servings*

# POLSKA KIELBASA SIMMERED IN BEER AND ONIONS

**4 tablespoons butter**
**4 onions, thinly sliced**
**1 pound HILLSHIRE FARM® Polska Kielbasa, diagonally sliced into ¼-inch pieces**
**1 bottle (12 ounces) beer**

Melt butter in large skillet over medium heat; sauté onions 4 to 5 minutes. Add Polska Kielbasa; brown 3 to 4 minutes on each side. Pour beer into skillet; bring to a boil. Reduce heat and simmer, uncovered, 25 minutes.

*Makes 4 to 6 servings*

## Quick Tip

For added flavor in this leg of lamb, soak sprigs of fresh rosemary in water for 10 to 15 minutes, then place them directly on the coals during the last 10 minutes of grilling.

# PEACHY PORK PICANTE

**4 boneless top loin pork chops, cubed**
**2 tablespoons taco seasoning**
**1 cup salsa**
**4 tablespoons peach preserves**

Toss pork with taco seasoning. Lightly brown pork in a nonstick skillet over medium-high heat; stir in salsa and preserves. Bring to a boil; lower heat. Cover and simmer 8 to 10 minutes. Serve with corn and black bean salad.

*Makes 4 servings*

*Favorite recipe from* **National Pork Board**

# RANCHERO RIBS

**1 can (21 ounces) peach pie filling or topping**
**1 can (15.5 ounces) HUNT'S® Manwich Original Sloppy Joe Sauce**
**2 pounds pork baby back ribs**
**½ teaspoon salt**

In medium bowl, combine pie filling and Manwich Sauce.

On baking sheet lined with foil, arrange ribs in single layer; season with salt. Brush both sides of ribs with Manwich Sauce mixture.

Bake at 350°F 1 hour, basting with accumulated juices every 20 minutes.

*Makes 4 servings*

## Quick Tip

Pork back ribs are meatier and less fatty than spareribs. Cook pork until it is barely pink in center (155° to 160°F on a meat thermometer).

# ORIENTAL FLANK STEAK

**¾ cup WISH-BONE® Italian Dressing***
**3 tablespoons soy sauce**
**3 tablespoons firmly packed brown sugar**
**½ teaspoon ground ginger (optional)**
**1 to 1½ pounds flank, top round or sirloin steak**

*\*Also terrific with Wish-Bone® Robusto Italian, Lite Italian or Red Wine Vinaigrette Dressing.*

In small bowl, combine all ingredients except steak.

In large, shallow nonaluminum baking dish or plastic bag, pour ½ cup marinade over steak. Cover, or close bag, and marinate in refrigerator, turning occasionally, 3 to 24 hours. Refrigerate remaining marinade.

Remove steak from marinade, discarding marinade. Grill or broil steak, turning once and brushing frequently with reserved marinade until steak is desired doneness.

*Makes about 4 servings*

TIP: When slicing cooked flank steak, it is always best to slice it across the grain and at a 45 deree angle. This will result in more tender and attractive slices.

**Prep Time:** 5 minutes
**Cook Time:** 15 minutes
**Marinate Time:** 3 hours

# PEACHY PORK ROAST

**1 (3- to 4-pound) rolled boneless pork loin roast**
**1 cup (12-ounce jar) SMUCKER'S® Currant Jelly**
**½ cup SMUCKER'S® Peach Preserves**
**Fresh peach slices and currants for garnish, if desired**

Place pork in roasting pan; insert meat thermometer into one end of roast. Bake at 325°F for 30 to 40 minutes or until browned. Turn roast and bake an additional 30 minutes to brown the bottom. Turn roast again and drain off drippings.

In saucepan over medium heat, melt currant jelly and peach preserves. Brush roast generously with sauce.

Continue baking until meat thermometer reads 160°F, about 15 minutes, basting occasionally with sauce.

Remove roast from oven. Garnish with peach slices and currants. Serve with remaining sauce.

*Makes 8 to 10 servings*

NOTE: Canned, sliced peaches can be substituted for fresh peaches.

# ROASTED PEPPERED PORK TENDERLOIN

**Boneless single loin pork roast, about 2 pounds**
**1 teaspoon garlic pepper spice blend**
**1 teaspoon dried rosemary, crushed**

Heat oven to 350°F. Coat roast with garlic-pepper and rosemary; place in shallow roasting pan and roast for 45 minutes, until meat thermometer inserted reads 150° to 155°F. Remove from oven and let rest for 5 to 10 minutes before slicing to serve.

*Makes 8 servings*

*Favorite recipe from **National Pork Board***

# HOME-STYLE BEEF BRISKET

**1 envelope LIPTON® RECIPE SECRETS® Onion Soup Mix***
**¾ cup water**
**½ cup ketchup**
**1 teaspoon garlic powder**
**½ teaspoon ground black pepper**
**1 (3-pound) boneless brisket of beef**

*\*Also terrific with LIPTON® RECIPE SECRETS® Onion Mushroom, Beefy Mushroom, Beefy Onion, Savory Herb with Garlic or Fiesta Herb with Red Pepper Soup Mix.*

1. Preheat oven to 325°F. In 13×9-inch baking or roasting pan, add soup mix blended with water, ketchup, garlic powder and pepper.

2. Add brisket; turn to coat.

3. Loosely cover with aluminum foil and bake 3 hours or until brisket is tender. If desired, thicken gravy.

*Makes 8 servings*

TIP: For a quick one-dish dinner, add ½ pound carrots, cut into 2-inch pieces and 1 pound potatoes, peeled, if desired, and cut into 2-inch chunks during last hour of baking.

# MAPLE-GLAZED HAM

**4 slices ham (3 ounces each)**
**¼ cup maple syrup**
**1 teaspoon Dijon mustard**

1. Preheat broiler.

2. Place ham slices on broiler pan. Combine syrup and mustard in small bowl. Brush each slice with about 1½ teaspoons of syrup mixture.

3. Broil 4 inches below heat about 4 minutes or until ham starts to brown. Turn and brush with remaining syrup mixture. Broil until browned. *Makes 4 servings*

## Express Recipe

Marinate flank steak prior to grilling in a combination of ½ cup soy sauce, 4 tablespoons olive oil, 3 tablespoons red wine vinegar and 2 teaspoons garlic pepper.

# ONION-MARINATED STEAK

**2 large red onions**
**1 cup plus 2 tablespoons WISH-BONE® Italian Dressing***
**1 (2- to 3-pound) boneless sirloin or London broil steak**

*\*Also terrific with Wish-Bone® Robusto Italian or Just 2 Good! Italian Dressing.*

Cut 1 onion in half; refrigerate one half. Chop remaining onion to equal 1½ cups. In blender or food processor, process 1 cup Italian dressing and chopped onion until puréed.

In large, shallow nonaluminum baking dish or plastic bag, pour 1¾ cups dressing-onion marinade over steak; turn to coat. Cover, or close bag, and marinate in refrigerator, turning occasionally, 3 to 24 hours. Refrigerate remaining ½ cup marinade.

Remove steak from marinade, discarding marinade. Grill or broil steak, turning and brushing frequently with refrigerated marinade, until steak is done.

Meanwhile, in saucepan, heat remaining 2 tablespoons Italian dressing and cook remaining onion half, cut into thin rings, stirring occasionally, 4 minutes or until tender. Serve over steak.                    *Makes 8 servings*

# ORIGINAL RANCH® PORK CHOPS

**1 packet (1 ounce) HIDDEN VALLEY® The Original Ranch®**
**Salad Dressing & Seasoning Mix**
**¼ teaspoon black pepper**
**6 pork chops (about ¾ inch thick)**
**Dash of paprika**

Combine salad dressing & seasoning mix and pepper. Rub mixture on both sides of pork chops. Arrange pork chops in a single layer in a shallow baking pan. Sprinkle with paprika. Bake at 450°F for 20 to 25 minutes or until cooked through.
                    *Makes 4 to 6 servings*

# SLOW COOKER MESQUITE BEEF

**1 boneless beef chuck roast (about 4 to 5 pounds)**
**1 cup LAWRY'S® Mesquite Marinade with Lime Juice,**
    **divided**
**French rolls, flour tortillas or taco shells (optional)**

Slow Cooker Directions
Trim fat from meat. Place meat in slow cooker. Pour ¾ cup
Mesquite Marinade over meat. Cover and cook on LOW for
9 to 10 hours. Remove meat to platter and shred with fork.
Return meat to slow cooker with juices; add remaining ¼ cup
Mesquite Marinade. Serve shredded beef in warmed French
rolls or in warmed flour tortillas or taco shells, if desired.
                                        *Makes 8 to 10 servings*

SERVING SUGGESTION: Add your favorite frozen stew
vegetables during the last hour of cooking for a pot
roast/stew meal.

**Prep Time:** 3 to 4 minutes
**Slow Cooker Time:** 9 to 10 hours

# MESQUITE & GARLIC GRILLED STEAK

**1½ pounds steak, 1-inch thick (top sirloin, rib-eye or T-bone)**
**1 bottle (12 ounces) LAWRY'S® Mesquite Marinade with**
    **Lime Juice**
**1½ teaspoons LAWRY'S® Seasoned Pepper**
**1 teaspoon LAWRY'S® Garlic Powder With Parsley**

Pierce steak and place in large resealable plastic bag. In
medium bowl, mix together Mesquite Marinade, Seasoned
Pepper and Garlic Powder With Parsley; reserve ⅓ cup
marinade mixture. Pour remaining marinade mixture into
bag with steak; seal bag. Marinate in refrigerator for
30 minutes, turning once. Remove steak from bag, discarding
used marinade. Grill, brushing often with reserved marinade
mixture, until desired degree of doneness, about 16 to
20 minutes.                              *Makes 4 to 6 servings*

**Prep Time:** 7 minutes
**Marinate Time:** 30 minutes
**Cook Time:** 16 to 20 minutes

## LEMON–CAPERED PORK TENDERLOIN

**1 boneless pork tenderloin (about 1½ pounds)**
**1 tablespoon crushed capers**
**1 teaspoon dried rosemary leaves, crushed**
**¼ cup lemon juice**

1. Preheat oven to 350°F. Trim fat from tenderloin; discard. Set tenderloin aside.

2. Combine capers, rosemary and ⅛ teaspoon black pepper in small bowl. Rub mixture over tenderloin. Place tenderloin in shallow roasting pan. Pour 1 cup water and lemon juice over tenderloin.

3. Bake, uncovered, 1 hour or until thermometer inserted into thickest part of tenderloin registers 160°F. Remove from oven; cover with foil. Allow to stand 10 minutes. Cut evenly into 8 slices before serving. Garnish as desired.

*Makes 8 servings*

## SOUTHWESTERN KABOBS

**4 boneless top loin pork chops, cut into 1-inch cubes**
**4 tablespoons taco or fajita seasoning**
**½ green bell pepper, seeded and cut into 1-inch pieces**
**½ large onion, peeled and cut into 1-inch pieces**

In a plastic food storage bag or shallow bowl, toss together pork cubes with desired seasoning until pork is evenly coated. Thread pork cubes, alternating with pepper and onion pieces, onto skewers.* Grill over a medium-hot fire, turning occasionally, until pork is nicely browned.

*Makes 4 servings*

*\*If using wooden skewers, soak in water for 20 minutes before using.*

*Favorite recipe from* **National Pork Board**

---

## Express Recipe

Prepare a quick and easy skillet dinner using just four ingredients. Brown 4 pork chops, seasoned with salt and pepper, in a medium nonstick skillet over medium heat. Remove the chops from the skillet. In the same skillet, prepare a 7-ounce package of Spanish rice mix according to the package directions, simmering the rice mixture 5 minutes, then top with 4 green bell pepper rings and the chops. Cover; cook until the rice is tender and the chops are cooked. Sprinkle with shredded Jack cheese.

# Speedy Poultry

## Quick Tip

Loosely 'crunch up' some foil in the baking dish around the chicken to keep grease from splattering in the oven. Also, elevate the chicken on a cooling rack in the dish to help brown the bottom of the chicken.

## LEMON ROSEMARY ROAST CHICKEN

1 whole chicken (about 4 to 4½ pounds)
2½ teaspoons LAWRY'S® Seasoned Salt
2 teaspoons whole dried rosemary, crumbled
1 teaspoon LAWRY'S® Lemon Pepper

Rinse chicken with cold water; pat dry with paper towels. In small bowl, combine Seasoned Salt, rosemary and Lemon Pepper. Gently lift skin from meat on breast. Rub seasoning mixture onto meat under skin, all over outside of chicken and inside cavity. Spray 13×9×2-inch baking dish with nonstick cooking spray; add chicken, breast-side-up. Roast in 400°F oven until meat is no longer pink and juices run clear when cut (175° to 180°F at thickest joint), about 60 to 70 minutes. Let stand 10 minutes before carving.

*Makes 8 servings*

**Prep Time:** 10 minutes
**Cook Time:** 60 to 70 minutes

## Express Recipe

Cut 3 chicken breasts into thin strips. Stir-fry chicken and 1 green bell pepper, cubed, in 1 tablespoon vegetable oil in a large skillet until it is no longer pink. Add 2 plums, cut into thin wedges and stir-fry 1 minute. Add ¾ cup sweet and sour sauce, stirring until hot. Serve over rice, if desired.

## HIDDEN VALLEY® FRIED CHICKEN

**1 broiler-fryer chicken, cut up (2 to 2½ pounds)**
**1 cup prepared HIDDEN VALLEY® The Original Ranch® Dressing**
**¾ cup all-purpose flour**
**1 teaspoon salt**
**½ teaspoon freshly ground black pepper**
**Vegetable oil**

Place chicken pieces in shallow baking dish; pour salad dressing over chicken. Cover; refrigerate at least 8 hours. Remove chicken. Shake off excess marinade; discard marinade. Preheat oven to 350°F. On plate, mix flour, salt and pepper; roll chicken in seasoned flour. Heat ½ inch oil in large skillet until small cube of bread dropped into oil browns in 60 seconds or until oil is 375°F. Fry chicken until golden, 5 to 7 minutes on each side; transfer to baking pan. Bake until chicken is tender and juices run clear, about 30 minutes. Serve with corn muffins, if desired.

*Makes 4 main-dish servings*

## LOUISIANA CHICKEN

**4 chicken breast halves, skinned and boned**
**2 cans (14½ ounces each) DEL MONTE® Diced Tomatoes with Green Pepper & Onion**
**2 tablespoons cornstarch**
**4 slices Monterey Jack cheese**
**Hot cooked rice (optional)**

1. Place chicken in baking dish. Cover and bake at 375°F, 30 to 35 minutes; drain.

2. Combine undrained tomatoes and cornstarch in saucepan; stir to dissolve cornstarch. Cook, stirring constantly, until thickened.

3. Remove chicken from baking dish. Pour all but 1 cup sauce into dish.

4. Arrange chicken over sauce in dish; top with remaining sauce. Place 1 slice cheese on each piece of chicken. Bake until cheese melts. Garnish with parsley. Serve with hot cooked rice, if desired.     *Makes 4 servings*

## ROAST TURKEY WITH HONEY CRANBERRY RELISH

**1 medium orange**
**12 ounces fresh or frozen whole cranberries**
**¾ cup honey**
**2 pounds sliced roasted turkey breast**

Quarter and slice unpeeled orange, removing seeds. Coarsely chop orange and cranberries. Place in medium saucepan and stir in honey. Bring to a boil over medium-high heat. Cook 3 to 4 minutes; cool. Serve over turkey.     *Makes 8 servings*

*Favorite recipe from* **National Honey Board**

## CHICKEN VEGETABLE SAUTÉ

**1 tablespoon vegetable oil**
**1½ pounds boneless skinless chicken breasts, cut into strips**
**1 bag (16 ounces) BIRDS EYE® frozen Farm Fresh Mixtures Sugar Snap Stir-Fry vegetables**
**⅔ cup LAWRY'S® Teriyaki Chicken Saute Sauce with Ginger and Sesame**
**⅓ cup slivered almonds, toasted**

• In large nonstick skillet, heat oil over medium heat.

• Add chicken; sauté about 8 minutes or until browned and no longer pink. Remove chicken; set aside.

• Add vegetables to skillet; sauté about 10 minutes or until crisp-tender.

• Return chicken to skillet; add teriyaki sauce. Stir to coat. Cook 2 to 3 minutes more or until heated through.

• Sprinkle with almonds.     *Makes 4 servings*

SERVING SUGGESTION: Serve over hot cooked rice.

**Prep Time:** 5 minutes
**Cook Time:** 20 minutes

---

## Quick Tip

Boneless chicken breasts are easier to cut into thin strips if they are slightly frozen. After slicing, allow the chicken to thaw completely before cooking it.

# Quick Tip

Always marinate chicken in the refrigerator. Marinating in resealable plastic bags makes cleanup easy.

## CARIBBEAN JERK CHICKEN WITH TROPICAL FRUIT SALSA

**1 cup plus 2 tablespoons LAWRY'S® Caribbean Jerk Marinade with Papaya Juice, divided**
**4 boneless, skinless chicken breasts**
**1 can (15¼ ounces) tropical fruit salad, drained**

In large resealable plastic bag, place ¾ cup Caribbean Jerk Marinade and chicken; seal bag. Marinate in refrigerator at least 30 minutes or up to 3 hours. Meanwhile, combine fruit salad with 2 tablespoons Marinade. Cover and chill in refrigerator. Remove chicken from bag, discarding used marinade. Grill or broil chicken, brushing often with remaining Marinade, until no longer pink and juices run clear when cut, about 13 to 20 minutes. Spoon fruit salsa over top of each cooked chicken breast before serving.

*Makes 4 servings*

**Prep Time:** 8 minutes
**Marinate Time:** 30 minutes to 3 hours
**Cook Time:** 13 to 20 minutes

## RASPBERRY-GLAZED TURKEY

**½ cup SMUCKER'S® Seedless Red Raspberry Jam**
**6 tablespoons raspberry vinegar**
**¼ cup Dijon mustard**
**4 small turkey breast tenderloins**

In large saucepan, stir together jam, vinegar and mustard. Bring to a boil over high heat; cook and stir 3 minutes. Reserve about ½ cup of glaze; coat turkey with some of remaining glaze.

Set turkey on rack in broiler pan. Broil about 4 inches from heat for 15 to 20 minutes or until no longer pink in center, turning and basting once with remaining glaze.

Slice turkey crosswise. Serve with reserved glaze.

*Makes 4 to 6 servings*

# SMOKED TURKEY WITH SUMMER CRANBERRY NECTAR

**1 BUTTERBALL® Fully Cooked Smoked Young Turkey, thawed, sliced thin**
**1 can (16 ounces) whole berry cranberry sauce**
**Juice of ½ lime**
**1 tablespoon seeded and chopped jalapeño pepper**
**½ teaspoon salt**

Combine cranberry sauce, lime juice, jalapeño pepper and salt in food processor; process until smooth. Spoon cranberry nectar over sliced turkey. *Makes 6 servings*

SERVING SUGGESTION: Serve with cranberry-studded mini-corn muffins.

**Prep Time: 15 minutes**

# HIDDEN VALLEY® CITRUS CHICKEN SUPPER

**1 packet (1 ounce) HIDDEN VALLEY® The Original Ranch® Salad Dressing & Seasoning Mix**
**1 pound boneless, skinless chicken breasts, cut into strips**
**1 tablespoon vegetable oil**
**⅓ cup chicken broth**
**3 tablespoons orange marmalade**

Sauté chicken in oil until browned. Combine dressing mix, broth and marmalade; pour on chicken. Cover and simmer 3 to 5 minutes. *Makes 4 servings*

SERVING SUGGESTION: Serve over rice; garnish with mandarin oranges.

# GOLDEN ONION–BAKED CHICKEN

**1 envelope LIPTON® RECIPE SECRETS® Golden Onion Soup Mix***
**½ cup plain dry bread crumbs**
**1 (2½- to 3-pound) chicken, cut into serving pieces**

*\*Also terrific with LIPTON® RECIPE SECRETS® Savory Herb with Garlic or Onion Soup Mix.*

1. Preheat oven to 375°F. In medium bowl, combine soup mix with bread crumbs. Moisten chicken with water, then dip in bread crumb mixture, coating well.

2. In large shallow baking pan arrange chicken; drizzle, if desired, with melted margarine or butter.

3. Bake uncovered 45 minutes or until chicken is thoroughly cooked.                                    *Makes 4 servings*

# SWEET & CRISPY OVEN–BAKED CHICKEN

**1 pound boneless skinless chicken breast halves**
**¼ cup *French's*® Sweet & Tangy Honey Mustard**
**1⅓ cups crushed *French's*® French Fried Onions**

1. Coat chicken with mustard. Dip into French Fried Onions. Place into lightly greased baking pan.

2. Bake at 400°F for 20 minutes or until no longer pink in center.                                    *Makes 4 servings*

**Prep Time:** 5 minutes
**Cook Time:** 20 minutes

## Quick Tip

To quickly crush French Fried Onions, place them in a large resealable plastic bag. Force the excess air out of the bag and seal it. Roll a rolling pin back and forth over the bag until the onions are evenly crushed.

## HERBED TURKEY BREAST WITH ORANGE SAUCE

**1 large onion, chopped**
**3 cloves garlic, minced**
**1 teaspoon dried rosemary**
**2 to 3 pounds boneless skinless turkey breast**
**1½ cups orange juice**

**Slow Cooker Directions**

1. Place onion in slow cooker. Combine garlic, rosemary and ½ teaspoon black pepper in small bowl; set aside. Cut slices about three fourths of the way through turkey at 2-inch intervals. Rub garlic mixture between slices.

2. Place turkey, cut side up, in slow cooker. Pour orange juice over turkey. Cover; cook on LOW 7 to 8 hours or until internal temperature reaches 170°F when tested with meat thermometer inserted into the thickest part of breast.

3. Transfer turkey to cutting board; cover with foil and let stand 10 to 15 minutes before carving. Internal temperature will rise 5° to 10°F during stand time. Serve sauce mixture from slow cooker with sliced turkey.

*Makes 4 to 6 servings*

## CHICKEN DIVAN

**¾ pound fresh broccoli, cut into flowerets *or* 1 package (10 ounces) frozen broccoli flowerets**
**2 cups shredded cooked chicken**
**1 cup prepared HIDDEN VALLEY® The Original Ranch® Dressing**
**1 tablespoon grated Parmesan cheese**
**Cherry tomatoes**

Preheat oven to 350°F. In medium saucepan, cook broccoli in boiling water to cover until tender, about 4 minutes. Drain thoroughly; place in shallow baking dish. Top with chicken and salad dressing. Sprinkle with Parmesan cheese. Cover loosely with foil; bake until heated through, about 15 minutes. Garnish with cherry tomatoes.

*Makes 4 servings*

## Express Recipe

To make lime and garlic flavored chicken, pound boneless skinless chicken breasts to ¼- to ½-inch thickness. Brown the chicken on both sides in a large nonstick skillet coated with cooking spray, then remove them from the pan. Add 1 tablespoon olive oil to the skillet and sauté 2 cloves of minced garlic and 1 bunch of thinly sliced green onions until they are tender. Return the chicken to the skillet and pour the juice of 1 lime over the chicken. Continue sautéing until the chicken is no longer pink in the center. Sprinkle with salt and black pepper before serving.

# CLASSIC FRIED CHICKEN

**¾ cup all-purpose flour**
**1 teaspoon salt**
**¼ teaspoon pepper**
**1 frying chicken (2½ to 3 pounds), cut up**
**½ cup CRISCO® Oil***

*\*Use your favorite Crisco Oil product.*

1. Combine flour, salt and pepper in paper or plastic bag. Add a few pieces of chicken at a time. Shake to coat.

2. Heat oil to 365°F in electric skillet or on medium-high heat in large heavy skillet. Fry chicken 30 to 40 minutes without lowering heat until no longer pink in center. Turn once for even browning. Drain on paper towels.

*Makes 4 servings*

SPICY FRIED CHICKEN: Increase pepper to ½ teaspoon. Combine pepper with ½ teaspoon poultry seasoning, ½ teaspoon paprika, ½ teaspoon cayenne pepper and ¼ teaspoon dry mustard. Rub on chicken before step 1. Substitute 2¼ teaspoons garlic salt, ¼ teaspoon salt and ¼ teaspoon celery salt for 1 teaspoon salt. Combine with flour in step 1 and proceed as directed above.

# CHICKY QUICKY

**1 cup SONOMA® Dried Tomato Bits**
**8 chicken thighs (or breast halves)**
**Juice of 1 lemon**
**1 tablespoon rosemary**
**Salt and pepper, to taste**

Place tomato bits in bottom of baking pan; arrange chicken in one layer on top of tomatoes. Squeeze lemon juice over chicken. Sprinkle rosemary, salt and pepper over chicken.

Cover and bake at 350°F until tender, about 40 to 45 minutes. Before serving, spoon juices over top of chicken.

*Makes 4 servings*

## Quick Tip

For a thicker crust on Classic Fried Chicken, increase the flour to 1½ cups. Shake damp chicken in the seasoned flour. Place it on waxed paper and let it stand for 5 to 20 minutes before frying.

# GRILLED TURKEY WITH ROASTED GARLIC GRILLED CORN

**1 (4½- to 9-pound) Li'l BUTTERBALL® Young Turkey, thawed, giblets removed**
**Vegetable oil**
**8 ears fresh corn in husks**
**1 whole bulb fresh garlic**
**Olive oil**

Prepare charcoal covered grill for indirect-heat cooking. Position foil drip pan in middle of bottom rack; place 25 to 30 briquettes along the outside of each lengthwise side of the drip pan. Burn briquettes until covered with gray ash, about 30 minutes. Place top rack in grill with handle openings over coals.

Turn wings back to hold neck skin in place. Return legs to tucked position if untucked. Brush turkey with vegetable oil to prevent skin from drying. Insert meat thermometer into thickest part of thigh not touching bone.

Place unstuffed turkey, breast up, in center of rack over drip pan. Cover grill and leave vents open. Add 6 to 8 briquettes to each side every hour or as needed to maintain heat. Cook turkey to an internal thigh temperature of 180°F and breast to 170°F. (A 4½- to 9-pound turkey will take about 1½ to 2½ hours.)

To prepare corn and garlic for grilling, leave corn in husks and soak in cold water for 30 minutes. Carefully pull back husks and remove silks, leaving husks attached. Smooth husks over corn to enclose. Cut ½ inch off tip of garlic bulb; drizzle garlic with olive oil and wrap tightly in foil. Place corn and garlic on grill for last 30 to 40 minutes of grilling.

Remove husks and serve corn; spread with melted butter and roasted garlic.                    *Makes 8 servings*

**Prep Time:** 30 minutes plus grilling time

## CRISPY OVEN-BAKED CHICKEN

**4 boneless skinless chicken breast halves (about
    4 ounces each)**
**¾ cup GUILTLESS GOURMET® Roasted Red Pepper Salsa
    Nonstick cooking spray**
**1 cup (3.5 ounces) crushed\* GUILTLESS GOURMET®
    Baked Tortilla Chips (yellow corn, red corn or chili
    lime)**
**Cherry tomatoes and pineapple sage leaves (optional)**

*\*Crush tortilla chips in the original bag or between two pieces of waxed
paper with a rolling pin.*

Wash chicken; pat dry with paper towels. Place chicken in
shallow nonmetal pan or place in large resealable plastic food
storage bag. Pour salsa over chicken. Cover with foil or seal
bag; marinate in refrigerator 8 hours or overnight.

Preheat oven to 350°F. Coat baking sheet with cooking spray.
Place crushed chips on waxed paper. Remove chicken from
salsa, discarding salsa; roll chicken in crushed chips. Place on
prepared baking sheet; bake 45 minutes or until chicken is
no longer pink in center and chips are crisp. Serve hot.
Garnish with tomatoes and sage, if desired.

*Makes 4 servings*

## TERIYAKI PLUM CHICKEN

**2 plums, finely chopped**
**½ cup LA CHOY® Teriyaki Sauce**
**½ cup plum jam**
**2 tablespoons WESSON® Vegetable Oil**
**1½ to 2 pounds chicken pieces**
**Fresh plum slices (optional)**

In a large bowl, combine *all* ingredients *except* chicken and
plum slices; mix well. Add chicken, cover and marinate in
refrigerator at least 2 hours. Place chicken on grill over
medium-hot coals. Grill, basting occasionally with marinade
and turning often, for 20 minutes or until meat is no longer
pink. Garnish with fresh plum slices, if desired.

*Makes 4 servings*

---

### Express Recipe

Place a 3-pound cut-up chicken in a 13×9-inch baking dish. Combine 1 cup apricot preserves, 3 tablespoons sherry and 3 tablespoons soy sauce; pour over the chicken. Bake in a preheated 325°F oven for 45 to 50 minutes, turning once.

# CUTLETS MILANESE

**1 package (about 1 pound) PERDUE® FIT 'N EASY®**
   **Thin-Sliced Turkey Breast Cutlets or Chicken Breast**
   **Salt and ground pepper to taste**
**½ cup Italian seasoned bread crumbs**
**½ cup grated Parmesan cheese**
**1 large egg beaten with 1 teaspoon water**
**2 to 3 tablespoons olive oil**

Season cutlets with salt and pepper. On wax paper, combine bread crumbs and Parmesan cheese. Dip cutlets in egg mixture and roll in bread crumb mixture. In large nonstick skillet over medium-high heat, heat oil. Add cutlets and sauté 3 minutes per side, until golden brown and cooked through.

*Makes 4 servings*

**Prep Time:** 6 to 8 minutes
**Cook Time:** 6 minutes

# THE ORIGINAL RANCH®
# BROILED CHICKEN

**1 packet (1 ounce) HIDDEN VALLEY® The Original Ranch®**
   **Salad Dressing & Seasoning Mix**
**2 tablespoons olive oil**
**1 tablespoon red wine vinegar**
**1 pound boneless, skinless chicken breasts and/or**
   **thighs**

Combine salad dressing & seasoning mix, oil and vinegar in a resealable plastic bag. Add chicken; shake, working mixture into meat. Marinate 1 hour in refrigerator. Broil chicken about 10 to 14 minutes total, turning once or until no longer pink in center.

*Makes 4 servings*

# FAJITA–SEASONED GRILLED CHICKEN

**2 skinless boneless chicken breasts (4 ounces each)**
**1 bunch green onions, ends trimmed**
**1 tablespoon olive oil**
**2 teaspoons fajita seasoning mix**

1. Preheat grill for direct cooking.

2. Meanwhile, brush chicken and green onions with oil. Sprinkle chicken on both sides with seasoning mix. Grill chicken and onions 6 to 8 minutes or until chicken is no longer pink in center.

3. Serve chicken with onions.          *Makes 2 servings*

# FRENCH COUNTRY TIDBITS

**1 pound boneless, skinless chicken breasts, cut into chunks**
**1 bottle (12 ounces) LAWRY'S® Dijon & Honey Marinade with Lemon Juice, divided**
**Wooden skewers**
**1 pound kielbasa (smoked sausage), sliced into ½-inch pieces**
**1 pound baby red potatoes, cooked and halved**

In large resealable plastic bag, combine chicken with ⅔ cup Dijon & Honey Marinade; seal bag and shake to coat. Marinate in refrigerator for at least 30 minutes. Remove chicken from bag, discarding used marinade. Thread onto skewers alternately with kielbasa and potatoes. Grill or broil until chicken is no longer pink and juices run clear when cut, about 10 to 15 minutes, turning once and brushing often with remaining Marinade.

*Makes 6 to 8 servings or appetizers for about 24*

HINT: Soak wooden skewers in water for about 30 minutes before using to help reduce burning.

**Prep Time:** 15 minutes
**Marinate Time:** 30 minutes
**Cook Time:** 10 to 15 minutes

*Quick Tip*

For a quick version of French Country Tidbits, make it without chicken, using an additional ½ pound *each* of potatoes and kielbasa.

## PENNE WITH ROASTED CHICKEN & VEGETABLES

**1 whole roasted chicken (about 2 pounds)**
**1 package (16 ounces) uncooked penne pasta**
**1 pound deli roasted vegetables, cut into bite-size strips**
**⅓ cup preshredded Parmesan cheese**

1. Remove chicken meat from bones and shred. Discard bones and skin.

2. Cook pasta according to package directions; drain and return to hot pan. Add chicken and vegetables; toss until mixture is heated through. Sprinkle with cheese and black pepper to taste.

*Makes 6 servings*

## CITRUS CHICKEN

**1 large orange**
**1 large lime***
**¾ cup WISH-BONE® Italian Dressing**
**6 boneless, skinless chicken breast halves (about 1½ pounds)**

*\*Substitution: Omit lime peel. Use 3 tablespoons lime juice.*

From the orange, grate enough peel to measure 1½ teaspoons and squeeze enough juice to measure ⅓ cup; set aside.

From the lime, grate enough peel to measure 1 teaspoon and squeeze enough juice to measure 3 tablespoons; set aside.

For marinade, combine Italian dressing, orange and lime juices and orange and lime peels. In large, shallow nonaluminum baking dish or plastic bag, pour ¾ cup marinade over chicken; turn to coat. Cover, or close bag, and marinate in refrigerator, turning occasionally, 30 minutes to 3 hours. Refrigerate remaining ½ cup marinade.

Remove chicken from marinade, discarding marinade. Grill or broil chicken, turning once and brushing frequently with refrigerated marinade, 12 minutes or until chicken is no longer pink in center.

*Makes 6 servings*

VARIATION: Also terrific with WISH-BONE® Robusto Italian or Just 2 Good! Italian Dressing.

---

# Quick Tip

Cook twice as much pasta as you need one night and get a head start on the next pasta meal. Thoroughly drain the pasta you are not using immediately and plunge it into a bowl of ice water to stop the cooking. Drain completely and toss it with 1 or 2 tablespoons of olive oil. Cover and refrigerate up to 3 days. To reheat the pasta, microwave on HIGH for 2 to 4 minutes, stirring halfway through.

## ROASTED CHICKEN AU JUS

**1 envelope LIPTON® RECIPE SECRETS® Onion Soup Mix\***
**2 tablespoons BERTOLLI® Olive Oil**
**1 (2½- to 3-pound) chicken, cut into serving pieces**
**½ cup hot water**

*\*Also terrific with LIPTON® RECIPE SECRETS® Savory Herb with Garlic, Onion Mushroom or Ranch Soup Mix.*

1. Preheat oven to 425°F. In large bowl, combine soup mix and oil; add chicken and toss until evenly coated.

2. In bottom of broiler pan without rack, arrange chicken. Roast chicken, basting occasionally, 40 minutes or until chicken is thoroughly cooked.

3. Remove chicken to serving platter. Add hot water to pan and stir, scraping brown bits from bottom of pan. Serve sauce over chicken.

*Makes 4 servings*

## APRICOT-GLAZED CHICKEN

**½ cup WISH-BONE® Italian Dressing\***
**2 teaspoons ground ginger (optional)**
**1 chicken, cut into serving pieces (2½ to 3 pounds)**
**¼ cup apricot or peach preserves**

*\*Also terrific with WISH-BONE® Robusto Italian Dressing.*

In large, shallow nonaluminum baking dish or plastic bag, blend Italian dressing and ginger. Add chicken; turn to coat. Cover, or close bag, and marinate in refrigerator, turning occasionally, 3 hours or overnight. Remove chicken, reserving ¼ cup marinade.

In small saucepan, bring reserved marinade to a boil and continue boiling 1 minute. Remove from heat and stir in preserves until melted; set aside.

Grill or broil chicken until chicken is thoroughly cooked near the bone, brushing with preserve mixture during last 5 minutes of cooking.

*Makes 4 servings*

---

## Quick Tip

For a slow cooker version of Roasted Chicken au Jus, rub chicken pieces with soup mix combined with oil. Place the chicken in a slow cooker. Cover. Cook on HIGH 4 hours or LOW 6 to 8 hours. Serve as directed.

## ROAST GARLIC CHICKEN

**1 whole broiler/fryer chicken (about 3 to 4 pounds)**
**2 tablespoons lemon juice**
**1½ teaspoons LAWRY'S® Garlic Powder With Parsley**
**2 teaspoons LAWRY'S® Seasoned Salt**

Sprinkle chicken with lemon juice, Garlic Powder With Parsley and Seasoned Salt over outside and inside cavity of chicken. Spray 13×9×2-inch baking dish and roasting rack with nonstick cooking spray. Place chicken breast-side-up on roasting rack. Roast in 400°F oven until meat is no longer pink and juices run clear when cut (175° to 180°F at thickest joint), about 60 to 70 minutes. Let stand 10 minutes before carving.                        *Makes 6 servings*

**Prep Time:** 10 minutes
**Cook Time:** 60 to 70 minutes

## GRILLED SUMMER
## CHICKEN & VEGETABLES

**1¼ cups WISH-BONE® Italian Dressing,* divided**
**4 chicken breast halves (about 2 pounds)**
**4 ears fresh or frozen corn (about 2 pounds)**
**2 large tomatoes, halved crosswise**

*\*Also terrific with WISH-BONE® Robusto Italian or Just 2 Good! Italian Dressing.*

In large, shallow nonaluminum baking dish, pour 1 cup Italian dressing over chicken, corn and tomatoes. Cover and marinate chicken and vegetables in refrigerator, turning occasionally, 3 to 24 hours.

Remove chicken and vegetables from marinade, discarding marinade. Grill or broil chicken and corn 20 minutes, turning and brushing frequently with remaining dressing. Arrange tomato halves, cut sides up, on grill or broiler pan and continue cooking chicken and vegetables, turning and brushing occasionally with dressing, 10 minutes or until chicken is thoroughly cooked in center and corn is tender.

*Makes 4 servings*

# CRISPY ONION CHICKEN FINGERS

**1⅓ cups *French's*® French Fried Onions**
**1 pound boneless skinless chicken fingers**
**3 to 4 tablespoons *French's*® Sweet & Tangy Honey Mustard**

1. Preheat oven to 400°F. Place French Fried Onions in resealable plastic food storage bag; seal. Crush onions with rolling pin.

2. Coat chicken fingers with mustard. Dip into crushed onions. Place chicken on baking sheet.

3. Bake 15 minutes or until chicken is crispy and no longer pink in center.　　*Makes 4 servings*

**Prep Time:** 10 minutes
**Cook Time:** 15 minutes

# ONION CRUMB CHICKEN CUTLETS

**1⅓ cups *French's*® French Fried Onions**
**4 thinly sliced chicken cutlets (1 pound), pounded to ¼-inch thickness**
**3 tablespoons *French's*® Bold n' Spicy Brown Mustard**
**1 to 2 tablespoons vegetable oil**
**Salt and pepper to taste**

Place French Fried Onions in resealable plastic food storage bag; seal. Press with rolling pin until onions are finely crushed. Transfer to sheet of waxed paper.

Brush each side of chicken with about 1 teaspoon mustard. Dip into crushed onions, pressing gently to coat.

Heat 1 tablespoon oil in large nonstick skillet over medium heat. Cook chicken, in batches, 1 to 2 minutes per side or until no longer pink in center. Repeat with remaining oil and cutlets. Season to taste with salt and pepper.

*Makes 4 servings*

**Prep Time:** 15 minutes
**Cook Time:** 4 to 8 minutes

# MAGICALLY MOIST CHICKEN

**1 pound boneless, skinless chicken breast halves**
**½ cup HELLMANN'S® or BEST FOODS® Real Mayonnaise**
**1¼ cups Italian seasoned dry bread crumbs**

1. Preheat oven to 425°F. Brush chicken on all sides with mayonnaise.

2. In large plastic bag or bowl place bread crumbs. Add chicken, one piece at a time; toss to coat. On rack in broiler pan or on foil-lined baking sheet, arrange chicken.

3. Bake 20 minutes or until chicken is golden brown and thoroughly cooked.                    *Makes 4 servings*

**Prep Time:** 5 minutes
**Cook Time:** 20 minutes

# SESAME HOISIN GLAZED CHICKEN

**½ cup plus 3 tablespoons LAWRY'S® Sesame Ginger**
**      Marinade with Mandarin Orange Juice, divided**
**2 pounds chicken thighs**
**1 tablespoon hoisin sauce**
**1 tablespoon honey**

In large resealable plastic bag, combine ½ cup Sesame Ginger Marinade with chicken; seal bag. Marinate in refrigerator for 30 minutes. Remove chicken from bag, discarding used marinade. Make glaze by whisking together remaining 3 tablespoons Marinade, hoisin sauce and honey. Place chicken, skin-side-up, on baking rack in foil-lined baking pan. Bake chicken in preheated 350°F oven, brushing with glaze several times, until chicken is no longer pink and juices run clear when cut, about 45 minutes.          *Makes 4 servings*

SERVING SUGGESTION: Serve over bed of hot cooked rice or noodles, garnished with toasted sesame seeds and green onions, if desired.

**Prep Time:** 3 to 5 minutes
**Marinate Time:** 30 minutes
**Cook Time:** 45 minutes

# HERB ROASTED TURKEY

**1 (12-pound) turkey, thawed if frozen**
**½ cup FLEISCHMANN'S® Original Margarine, softened, divided**
**1 tablespoon Italian seasoning**

1. Remove neck and giblets from turkey cavities. Rinse turkey; drain well and pat dry. Free legs from tucked position; do not cut band of skin. Using rubber spatula or hand, loosen skin over breast, starting at body cavity opening by legs.

2. Blend 6 tablespoons margarine and Italian seasoning. Spread 2 tablespoons herb mixture inside body cavity; spread remaining herb mixture on meat under skin. Hold skin in place at opening with wooden picks. Return legs to tucked position; turn wings back to hold neck skin in place.

3. Place turkey, breast-side up, on flat rack in shallow open pan. Insert meat thermometer deep into thickest part of thigh next to body, not touching bone. Melt remaining 2 tablespoons margarine; brush over skin.

4. Roast at 325°F for 3½ to 3¾ hours. When skin is golden brown, cover breast loosely with foil to prevent overbrowning. Check for doneness; thigh temperature should be 180° to 185°F. Transfer turkey to cutting board; let stand 15 to 20 minutes before carving. Remove wooden toothpicks just before carving.                    *Makes 12 servings*

**Preparation Time:** 20 minutes
**Cook Time:** 3 hours and 30 minutes
**Cooling Time:** 15 minutes
**Total Time:** 4 hours and 5 minutes

## Quick Tip

Oil and vinegar-based salad dressings make good marinades for chicken. Try Italian dressing, raspberry or balsamic vinaigrette.

# GRILLED ROSEMARY CHICKEN

**2 tablespoons lemon juice**
**2 cloves garlic, minced**
**2 tablespoons minced fresh rosemary**
**4 boneless skinless chicken breasts**

1. Whisk together lemon juice, 2 tablespoons olive oil, garlic, rosemary and ¼ teaspoon salt in small bowl. Pour into shallow glass dish. Add chicken, turning to coat both sides with lemon juice mixture. Cover and marinate in refrigerator 15 minutes, turning chicken once.

2. Grill chicken over medium-hot coals 5 to 6 minutes per side or until chicken is no longer pink in center.

*Makes 4 servings*

**Prep and Cook Time:** 30 minutes

# COUNTRY SMOTHERED CHICKEN

**1 (3- to 4-pound) chicken, cut up and skinned, if desired**
**1 onion, sliced crosswise into rings**
**1 green bell pepper, chopped**
**¼ cup *Frank's® RedHot®* Original Cayenne Pepper Sauce**

1. Place chicken into plastic or brown paper bag. Combine *3 tablespoons flour* with *1 teaspoon salt* and *½ teaspoon black pepper*. Sprinkle over chicken pieces. Close bag; shake bag to coat evenly. Heat *1 tablespoon oil* in large nonstick skillet until hot. Add chicken; cook 10 minutes or until browned on both sides. Transfer to dish. Drain off all but 1 tablespoon fat. Add onion and bell pepper; cook and stir 3 minutes or until tender.

2. Slowly add *1 cup water* and *Frank's RedHot* Sauce; stir until well blended. Heat to boiling. Return chicken to skillet. Reduce heat to medium-low. Cook, partially covered, 20 minutes or until chicken is no longer pink near bone. Serve with hot cooked noodles, if desired.

*Makes 6 servings*

**Prep Time:** 5 minutes
**Cook Time:** 35 minutes

## CRISPY ONION CHICKEN

**1⅓ cups *French's*® French Fried Onions**
**2 to 3 tablespoons *French's*® Sweet & Tangy Honey Mustard**
**4 to 6 boneless skinless chicken breast halves**

1. Preheat oven to 350°F. Place French Fried Onions in plastic bag. Press with rolling pin until onions are lightly crushed. Transfer to sheet of waxed paper.

2. Spread mustard evenly on chicken. Coat with onion crumbs; pressing gently to adhere.

3. Place in baking pan. Bake 20 minutes or until chicken is no longer pink in center.          *Makes 4 to 6 servings*

**Prep Time:** 10 minutes
**Cook Time:** 20 minutes

## PERFECT OVEN "FRIED" CHICKEN

**2 tablespoons LAWRY'S® Perfect Blend Seasoning and Rub for Chicken & Poultry**
**½ cup light mayonnaise**
**4 boneless, skinless chicken breasts**
**5 cups crushed corn flake cereal**

Preheat oven to 400°F. In large Ziploc® bag, mix Perfect Blends with mayonnaise. Add chicken to bag and shake until completely coated. Place corn flakes in another large Ziploc® bag; seal and crush. Drop chicken, one piece at a time, into crushed flakes and shake to coat. Set cooling rack on foil-lined baking sheet; spray with nonstick cooking spray. Place chicken on rack and bake until no longer pink and juices run clear when cut, about 35 minutes.

*Makes 4 servings*

SERVING SUGGESTION: Serve this delicious chicken with mashed potatoes, fries or tater tots. Add a crisp green salad to complete this quick and easy meal.

**Prep Time:** 10 minutes
**Cook Time:** 35 minutes

# FRESCO MARINATED CHICKEN

**1 envelope LIPTON® RECIPE SECRETS® Savory Herb
    with Garlic Soup Mix***
**⅓ cup water**
**¼ cup BERTOLLI® Olive Oil**
**1 teaspoon lemon juice or vinegar**
**4 boneless, skinless chicken breast halves (about
    1¼ pounds)**

*\*Also terrific with LIPTON® RECIPE SECRETS® Golden Onion Soup Mix.*

1. For marinade, blend all ingredients except chicken.

2. In shallow baking dish or plastic bag, pour ½ cup of the marinade over chicken. Cover, or close bag, and marinate in refrigerator, turning occasionally, up to 3 hours. Refrigerate remaining marinade.

3. Remove chicken, discarding marinade. Grill or broil chicken, turning once and brushing with refrigerated marinade until chicken is no longer pink in center.

*Makes 4 servings*

# SWEET 'N' TANGY GLAZED CHICKEN

**⅓ cup *Frank's® RedHot®* Original Cayenne Pepper Sauce**
**⅓ cup *French's®* Bold n' Spicy Brown Mustard *or* Napa
    Valley Style Dijon Mustard**
**⅓ cup honey**
**3 pounds chicken parts**

1. Preheat oven to 400°F. Combine *Frank's RedHot* Sauce, mustard and honey in a well-greased 3-quart baking dish.

2. Dip chicken pieces in mixture; arrange skin-side up in single layer. Bake 45 minutes or until chicken is no longer pink near bone, basting occasionally.

3. Serve chicken with sauce from pan.    *Makes 4 servings*

**Prep Time:** 5 minutes
**Cook Time:** 45 minutes

## CRISPY RANCH CHICKEN

**1½ cups cornflake crumbs
1 teaspoon dried rosemary
1½ cups ranch salad dressing
3 pounds chicken pieces (breasts, legs, thighs)**

Preheat oven to 375°F. Combine cornflakes, rosemary, ½ teaspoon salt and ½ teaspoon black pepper in medium bowl.

Pour salad dressing in separate medium bowl. Dip chicken pieces in salad dressing, coating well. Dredge coated chicken in crumb mixture.

Place in 13×9-inch baking dish coated with nonstick cooking spray. Bake 50 to 55 minutes or until juices run clear; serve with desired side dishes.      *Makes 6 servings*

## VEGGIE & CHICKEN NUGGETS

**1 bag (16 ounces) BIRDS EYE® frozen Farm Fresh
   Mixtures Broccoli, Cauliflower & Carrots
1 box (5½ ounces) seasoning & coating mix for chicken
   (2 packets)
¼ to ½ teaspoon garlic powder
1 pound boneless skinless chicken breast halves, cut
   into 1½- to 2-inch pieces**

• Preheat oven to 400°F.

• Rinse vegetables under warm water to thaw; drain.

• In small bowl, mix coating mix with garlic powder; place ½ of mixture in resealable plastic food storage bag. Add vegetables; shake until evenly coated. Place in single layer on ungreased 15×10-inch baking pan.

• Moisten chicken with water. Add remaining coating mixture and chicken to same bag; shake until evenly coated.

• Place chicken on pan with vegetables, using additional baking pan if too crowded.

• Bake 10 to 15 minutes or until chicken is no longer pink in center.      *Makes 4 servings*

**Prep Time:** 5 minutes
**Cook Time:** 15 minutes

---

**Quick Tip**

To add an Italian flare to Crispy Ranch Chicken, try substituting 1½ cups Italian-seasoned dried bread crumbs and ½ cup grated Parmesan cheese for the cornflake crumbs, rosemary, salt and pepper. Prepare the recipe as directed.

## THE ORIGINAL RANCH®
## CRISPY CHICKEN

**¼ cup unseasoned bread crumbs or corn flake crumbs**
**1 packet (1 ounce) HIDDEN VALLEY® The Original Ranch®**
**Salad Dressing & Seasoning Mix**
**6 bone-in chicken pieces**

Combine bread crumbs and salad dressing & seasoning mix in a resealable plastic bag. Add chicken pieces; seal bag. Shake to coat chicken. Bake chicken on an ungreased baking sheet at 375°F for 50 minutes or until no longer pink in center and juices run clear.          *Makes 4 to 6 servings*

## MARINATE WHILE
## YOU BAKE CHICKEN

**3 pounds chicken parts**
**1 cup LAWRY'S® Marinade with Fruit Juice**

Preheat oven to 375°F. Spray 13×9×2-inch glass baking dish with nonstick cooking spray. Place chicken in dish, skin-side-down. Pour Marinade over chicken and bake 30 minutes; turn chicken over and spoon Marinade in dish over each piece. Continue baking until meat is no longer pink and juices run clear when cut (175° to 185°F at thickest point), about 25 to 30 minutes. Spoon pan juices over chicken before serving.          *Makes 4 to 6 servings*

MEAL IDEA: May substitute 3 pounds chicken drummettes for chicken parts and bake at 450°F for 20 minutes, turn and brush with Marinade then cook for 20 minutes longer. Makes great appetizers and 'finger food' for kids.

VARIATIONS: Any of the following LAWRY'S® Marinades are excellent in this recipe—Herb & Garlic Marinade with Lemon Juice, Teriyaki Marinade with Pineapple Juice, Dijon & Honey Marinade with Lemon Juice, Caribbean Jerk Marinade with Papaya Juice, Mesquite Marinade with Lime Juice, Lemon Pepper Marinade with Lemon Juice

**Prep Time:** 4 minutes
**Cook Time:** 55 to 60 minutes

## MAPLE-GLAZED TURKEY BREAST

**1 bone-in turkey breast (5 to 6 pounds)**
**¼ cup pure maple syrup**
**1 tablespoon bourbon (optional)**
**2 teaspoons freshly grated orange peel**

1. Prepare barbecue grill with rectangular foil drip pan. Bank briquets on either side of drip pan for indirect cooking.

2. Insert meat thermometer into center of thickest part of turkey breast, not touching bone. Place turkey, bone side down, on roast rack or directly on grid, directly over drip pan. Grill turkey, on covered grill, over medium coals 55 minutes, adding 4 to 9 briquets to both sides of fire after 45 minutes to maintain medium coals.

3. Combine maple syrup, 2 tablespoons melted butter, bourbon and orange peel in small bowl; brush half of mixture over turkey. Continue to grill, covered, 10 minutes. Brush with remaining mixture; continue to grill, covered, about 10 minutes or until thermometer registers 170°F.

4. Transfer turkey to carving board; tent with foil. Let stand 10 minutes before carving. Cut turkey into thin slices. Garnish, if desired.          *Makes 6 to 8 servings*

VARIATION: For hickory-smoked flavor, cover 2 cups hickory chips with cold water; soak 20 minutes. Drain; sprinkle over coals just before placing turkey on grid.

## HONEY MUSTARD PECAN CHICKEN

**4 boneless skinless chicken breast halves**
**¼ cup *French's*® Sweet & Tangy Honey Mustard**
**1 cup finely chopped pecans**

1. Preheat oven to 400°F. Spread mustard evenly on chicken. Coat with pecans pressing gently to adhere.

2. Place chicken in greased and foil-lined baking pan. Bake 20 minutes or until chicken is no longer pink in center. Serve with additional mustard.          *Makes 4 servings*

**Prep Time:** 10 minutes
**Cook Time:** 20 minutes

## Quick Tip

Before grating the peel of citrus fruit, scrub it well with soap and water, then rinse well. Grate only the colored part of the peel, avoiding the bitter white pith underneath. The oil, which is the flavorful part of the peel, dissipates quickly, so the peel should be grated just before you use it.

# Simple Seafood

## SKILLET SHRIMP SCAMPI

**2 teaspoons BERTOLLI® Olive Oil**
**2 pounds uncooked shrimp, peeled and deveined**
**⅔ cup LAWRY'S® Herb & Garlic Marinade with Lemon Juice**
**¼ cup finely chopped green onion, including tops**

In large nonstick skillet, heat oil over medium heat. Add shrimp and Herb & Garlic Marinade. Cook, stirring often until shrimp turn pink, about 3 to 5 minutes. Stir in green onions.                                        *Makes 4 to 6 servings*

SERVING SUGGESTION: Serve over hot, cooked rice, orzo or your favorite pasta.

VARIATIONS: This dish is wonderful as an appetizer—serve it chilled with toothpicks. Or toss chilled scampi with pasta or a green salad for your next picnic. It is also delicious prepared with LAWRY'S® Lemon Pepper Marinade with Lemon Juice.

**Prep Time:** 5 minutes
**Cook Time:** 3 to 5 minutes

## *Quick Tip*

Most large supermarkets handle fresh fish. It's best to purchase fish on the day it is delivered to the store—ask the attendant at the fish counter about delivery days. In addition, you should try to cook fresh fish on the day you purchase it. If you must store it overnight, place the package on ice in the coldest part of the refrigerator.

## SWEET & ZESTY FISH WITH FRUIT SALSA

¼ cup *French's*® Bold n' Spicy Brown Mustard
¼ cup honey
2 cups chopped assorted fresh fruit (pineapple, kiwi, strawberries and mango)
1 pound sea bass or cod fillets or other firm-fleshed white fish

1. Preheat broiler or grill. Combine mustard and honey. Stir *2 tablespoons* mustard mixture into fruit; set aside.

2. Brush remaining mustard mixture on both sides of fillets. Place in foil-lined broiler pan. Broil (or grill) fish 6 inches from heat for 8 minutes or until fish is opaque.

3. Serve fruit salsa with fish.      *Makes 4 servings*

TIP: To prepare this meal even faster, purchase cut-up fresh fruit from the salad bar.

**Prep Time:** 15 minutes
**Cook Time:** 8 minutes

## BAKED SALMON

1 (4-ounce) salmon fillet
1 teaspoon fresh lemon juice
½ teaspoon Cajun seasoning mix

1. Preheat oven to 325°F.

2. Rinse salmon fillet and pat dry. Place fillet in center of large triangle of parchment paper on baking sheet. Sprinkle fillet with lemon juice and seasoning.

3. Double fold sides and ends of parchment paper to form packet, leaving head space for heat circulation. Bake 20 to 25 minutes. Carefully open packet to allow steam to escape. Salmon is done when it flakes easily with fork.

*Makes 1 serving*

**8 to 12 large sea scallops, halved crosswise**
**Salt and freshly ground black pepper, to taste**
**3 tablespoons FLEISCHMANN'S® Original Margarine,**
**divided**
**2 tomatoes, peeled, seeded and chopped**
**2 tablespoons chopped fresh *or* 2 teaspoons dried**
**basil leaves**

1. Dry scallops with paper towels; season with salt and pepper.

2. Heat 2 tablespoons margarine in large nonstick skillet over medium-high heat.

3. Arrange half the scallops in a single layer in skillet; cook for 1 to 2 minutes on each side or just until cooked. Transfer scallops to a platter; keep warm. Repeat with remaining scallops; remove to serving platter.

4. Melt remaining margarine in same skillet over medium-high heat. Add tomatoes and basil; heat through.

5. Spoon tomato mixture over the scallops; serve immediately.                *Makes 2 servings*

**Prep Time:** 10 minutes
**Cook Time:** 5 minutes
**Total Time:** 15 minutes

## CHILI GARLIC PRAWNS

**2 tablespoons vegetable oil**
**1 pound prawns, peeled and deveined**
**3 tablespoons LEE KUM KEE® Chili Garlic Sauce**
**1 green onion, cut into slices**

1. Heat oil in wok or skillet.

2. Add prawns and stir-fry until just pink.

3. Add chili garlic sauce and stir-fry until prawns are completely cooked.

4. Sprinkle with green onion and serve.    *Makes 4 servings*

## Quick Tip

To devein shrimp, make a small cut along the back and lift out the dark vein with the tip of a knife. This is easier to do under cold running water.

# GRILLED TEQUILA LIME SALMON

**1 cup LAWRY'S® Tequila Lime Marinade with Lime Juice, divided**
**1 pound fresh salmon fillet or steaks**
**1 lime, cut into wedges (optional garnish)**
**Fresh cilantro sprigs (optional garnish)**

In large resealable plastic bag, combine ¾ cup Tequila Lime Marinade and salmon, seal bag. Marinate in refrigerator for 30 minutes, turning occasionally. Remove salmon from bag, discarding used marinade. Grill salmon until opaque and fish begins to flake easily, 8 to 10 minutes, brushing often with remaining Marinade. Serve with lime wedges and fresh cilantro for garnish, if desired.          *Makes 4 servings*

SERVING SUGGESTION: Serve with black beans, rice and warm tortillas.

**Prep Time:** 5 minutes
**Marinate Time:** 30 minutes
**Cook Time:** 8 to 10 minutes

# WASABI SALMON

**2 tablespoons soy sauce**
**1½ teaspoons wasabi paste or powder, divided, plus more to taste**
**4 salmon fillets (6 ounces each) with skin**
**¼ cup mayonnaise**

1. Prepare grill or preheat broiler. Combine soy sauce and ½ teaspoon wasabi paste; mix well. Spoon mixture over salmon. Place salmon, skin sides down, on grid over medium coals or on rack of broiler pan. Grill on covered grill or broil 4 to 5 inches from heat source 8 minutes or until salmon is opaque in center.

2. Meanwhile, combine mayonnaise and remaining 1 teaspoon wasabi paste; mix well. Taste and add more wasabi if desired. Transfer salmon to serving plates; top with mayonnaise mixture.          *Makes 4 servings*

TIP: Wasabi comes from the root of an Asian plant. It is sometimes referred to as Japanese horseradish. When mixed with mayonnaise, it has a fiery sharp flavor.

---

*Quick Tip*

Always rinse fish fillets and steaks before cooking them. Rinsing removes dirt, bone fragments and loose scales. Pat the fish with paper towels until it is dry.

## Express Recipe

For flavorful grilled shrimp, combine ⅔ cup orange juice, 1 tablespoon lemon juice, 1 tablespoon soy sauce and 1 teaspoon dark sesame oil in a large resealable plastic food storage bag. Add 20 peeled, deveined jumbo shrimp and marinate them in the refrigerator for 30 minutes. Drain the shrimp and thread 5 of them onto each of 4 skewers. Grill the shrimp over medium heat about 6 minutes, turning once, until they are pink and opaque.

# MUSTARD–GRILLED RED SNAPPER

**½ cup Dijon mustard**
**1 tablespoon red wine vinegar**
**1 teaspoon ground red pepper**
**4 red snapper fillets (about 6 ounces each)**
**Fresh parsley sprigs and red peppercorns (optional)**

Spray grid with nonstick cooking spray. Prepare grill for direct cooking.

Combine mustard, vinegar and pepper in small bowl; mix well. Coat fish thoroughly with mustard mixture.

Place fish on grid. Grill, covered, over medium-high heat 8 minutes or until fish flakes easily when tested with fork, turning halfway through grilling time. Garnish with parsley sprigs and red peppercorns, if desired.     *Makes 4 servings*

# GRILLED SESAME GINGER SALMON

**1¼ cups LAWRY'S® Sesame Ginger Marinade with Mandarin Orange Juice, divided**
**1½ pounds salmon fillets**

In large resealable plastic bag, combine 1 cup Sesame Ginger Marinade and fish; seal bag. Marinate in refrigerator for 30 minutes. Remove fish from bag, discarding used marinade. Lightly oil grill grates. Cook fish on grill, brushing often with remaining Marinade, about 5 to 7 minutes per side, until fish is opaque and begins to flake easily.     *Make 4 servings*

SERVING SUGGESTION: Serve with your favorite rice side dish and grilled vegetables.

**Prep Time:** 4 minutes
**Marinate Time:** 30 minutes
**Cook Time:** 10 to 14 minutes (depends on thickness of fish)

# GARLIC SKEWERED SHRIMP

**1 pound raw large shrimp, peeled and deveined**
**2 tablespoons reduced-sodium soy sauce**
**3 cloves garlic, minced**
**¼ teaspoon red pepper flakes (optional)**
**3 green onions, cut into 1-inch pieces**

1. Prepare grill or preheat broiler. Soak 4 (12-inch) wooden skewers in water 25 to 30 minutes. Meanwhile, place shrimp in large plastic resealable food storage bag. Combine soy sauce, 1 tablespoon vegetable oil, garlic and red pepper, if desired, in cup; mix well. Pour over shrimp. Seal bag; turn to coat. Marinate at room temperature 15 minutes.

2. Drain shrimp; reserve marinade. Alternately thread shrimp and onions onto skewers. Place skewers on grid or rack of broiler pan. Brush with reserved marinade; discard any remaining marinade. Grill, covered, over medium-hot coals or broil 5 to 6 inches from heat 5 minutes on each side or until shrimp are pink and opaque. Serve on lettuce-lined plates, if desired. *Makes 4 servings*

SERVING SUGGESTION: For a more attractive presentation, leave the tails on the shrimp.

# GRILLED SALMON FILLETS

**1 tablespoon MRS. DASH® Lemon Pepper seasoning**
**2 tablespoons whole grain Dijon mustard**
**3 tablespoons olive oil**
**6 (6-ounce) salmon fillets**

In a bowl, mix together Mrs. Dash Lemon Pepper seasoning, whole grain Dijon mustard and olive oil. Rub this mixture into the salmon fillets. Place salmon in glass dish and refrigerate for 1 hour. Preheat grill to medium high. Place fillets skin side down and cook 5 to 6 minutes; turn carefully and continue cooking another 5 to 6 minutes. Serve immediately. *Makes 6 servings*

**Preparation Time:** 10 minutes
**Cooking Time:** 10 minutes

# NUTTY PAN-FRIED TROUT

**2 tablespoons oil**
**4 trout fillets (about 6 ounces each)**
**½ cup seasoned bread crumbs**
**½ cup pine nuts**

1. Heat oil in large skillet over medium heat. Lightly coat fish with crumbs. Add to skillet.

2. Cook 8 minutes or until fish flakes easily when tested with fork, turning after 5 minutes. Remove fish from skillet. Place on serving platter; keep warm.

3. Add nuts to drippings in skillet. Cook and stir 3 minutes or until nuts are lightly toasted. Sprinkle over fish.

*Makes 4 servings*

# LOUISIANA STIR-FRY

**2 tablespoons vegetable oil**
**1 pound raw medium shrimp, shelled and deveined, *or***
**    ½ pound sea scallops**
**1 bag (16 ounces) BIRDS EYE® frozen Farm Fresh**
**    Mixtures Broccoli, Corn & Red Peppers**
**½ green bell pepper, chopped**
**2 teaspoons water**
**1 can (14½ ounces) stewed tomatoes, drained**

• In wok or large skillet, heat oil over medium-high heat.

• Add shrimp; stir-fry 2 to 3 minutes or until shrimp turn pink and opaque. Remove to serving plate.

• Add vegetables, pepper and water to wok; cover and cook 4 to 6 minutes.

• Uncover; stir in tomatoes. Cook 3 to 4 minutes or until heated through and slightly thickened.

• Return shrimp to wok; cook and stir about 1 minute or until heated through.          *Makes 4 servings*

SERVING SUGGESTION: Stir ¼ teaspoon hot pepper sauce into stir-fry and serve over hot cooked rice.

**Prep Time:** 15 minutes
**Cook Time:** 12 to 15 minutes

## Quick Tip

You may substitute 1 package (16 ounces) frozen fully cooked shrimp or 1 pound imitation crab legs for the raw shrimp in Louisiana Stir-Fry. Add them to the cooked vegetables and cook until they are heated through.

# VERMOUTH SALMON

**2 (10×10-inch) sheets heavy-duty foil**
**2 salmon fillets or steaks (3 ounces each)**
   **Salt and black pepper**
**4 sprigs fresh dill (optional)**
**2 slices lemon**
**1 tablespoon vermouth**

1. Preheat oven to 375°F. Turn up the edges of 1 sheet of foil so juices will not run out. Place salmon in the center of the foil. Sprinkle with salt and pepper. Place dill, if desired, on top of salmon and lemon slices on top of the dill. Pour vermouth evenly over fish pieces.

2. Cover fish with second sheet of foil. Crimp edges of foil together to seal packet. Place packet on baking sheet. Bake 20 to 25 minutes or until salmon flakes easily when tested with fork.                    *Makes 2 servings*

# SEASONED FLORIDA GROUPER

**1½ pounds Florida grouper fillets**
**2 teaspoons paprika**
**1 teaspoon salt**
**1 teaspoon minced garlic**
**½ teaspoon white pepper**
**3 tablespoons vegetable oil**

Cut grouper fillets into four serving-size portions. Combine paprika, salt, garlic and pepper; mix well. Coat grouper with seasonings on all sides; set aside. Heat vegetable oil to medium-high in a large skillet. Place seasoned grouper in hot oil. Cook for about 3 minutes on each side, turning once.

*Makes 4 servings*

*Favorite recipe from Florida Department of Agriculture and Consumer Services, Bureau of Seafood and Aquaculture*

## SHRIMP AND VEGETABLES WITH LO MEIN NOODLES

**2 tablespoons vegetable oil**
**1 pound medium shrimp, peeled**
**2 packages (21 ounces each) frozen lo mein stir-fry mix with sauce**
  **Fresh cilantro (optional)**
**1 small wedge cabbage**
**¼ cup peanuts, chopped**

1. Heat oil in wok or large skillet over medium-high heat. Add shrimp; stir-fry 3 minutes or until shrimp are pink and opaque. Remove shrimp from wok to medium bowl. Set aside.

2. Remove sauce packet from stir-fry mix. Add frozen vegetables and noodles to wok; stir in sauce. Cover and cook 7 to 8 minutes, stirring frequently.

3. While vegetable mixture is cooking, chop enough cilantro to measure 2 tablespoons. Shred cabbage.

4. Stir shrimp, cilantro, if desired, and peanuts into vegetable mixture; heat through. Serve immediately with cabbage.

*Makes 6 servings*

**Prep and Cook Time:** 20 minutes

## GRILLED FRESH FISH

**3 to 3½ pounds fresh tuna or catfish**
**¾ cup prepared HIDDEN VALLEY® The Original Ranch® Dressing**
**Chopped fresh dill**
**Lemon wedges (optional)**

Place fish on heavy-duty foil. Cover with salad dressing. Grill over medium-hot coals until fish turns opaque and flakes easily when tested with fork, 20 to 30 minutes. Or, broil fish 15 to 20 minutes. Sprinkle with dill; garnish with lemon wedges, if desired.

*Makes 6 servings*

## BRONZED FISH

**3 tablespoons unsalted butter, melted
4 (4½-ounce) fish fillets, each about ½ to ¾ inch thick at thickest part
About 1 tablespoon plus 1 teaspoon Chef Paul Prudhomme's Seafood Magic®, Chef Paul Prudhomme's Blackened Redfish Magic®, or Chef Paul Prudhomme's Meat Magic®**

Place a heavy nonstick skillet over medium-high heat until hot, about 7 minutes.

As soon as skillet is hot, lightly coat one side of each fillet with butter, then sprinkle each buttered side evenly with ½ teaspoon of the seasoning of your choice. Place the fish in skillet, seasoned sides down, and sprinkle the top side of all the fillets evenly with the remaining seasoning.

Cook until the undersides of the fillets are bronze in color, about 2½ minutes. As the fish cooks, look for a white line coming up the side of each fillet as it turns from translucent to opaque. When one half of the thickness is opaque, turn the fish and cook approximately 2½ minutes longer. *Do not overcook.* The fish will continue to cook even after you remove it from the heat. Serve immediately.

*Makes 4 servings*

## SAVORY BAKED FISH

**6 boneless fish fillets, such as scrod, flounder or other mild white fish (about 8 ounces each)
¾ cup HIDDEN VALLEY® The Original Ranch® Dressing
Julienned vegetables, cooked (optional)**

Arrange fish fillets in a large oiled baking pan. Spread each fillet with 2 tablespoons dressing. Bake at 375°F for 10 to 20 minutes, depending on thickness of fish, or until fish flakes when tested with a fork. Finish under broiler to brown top. Serve on julienned vegetables, if desired.

*Makes 6 servings*

## Express Recipe

For a quick Shrimp Sauté, melt 2 tablespoons butter in a large skillet. Cook and stir ½ cup diced red bell pepper until tender. Add shrimp and sauté about 5 minutes or until they are pink and opaque. Stir in ¼ cup dry bread crumbs combined with ½ cup grated Parmesan cheese and ¼ teaspoon garlic pepper. Heat just until the cheese is melted.

## SAVORY SALMON

**6 small salmon steaks (about 6 ounces each)**
**¾ cup prepared HIDDEN VALLEY® The Original Ranch® Dressing**
**2 teaspoons chopped fresh dill *or* ¼ teaspoon dried dill weed**
**1 teaspoon chopped fresh parsley**
**Lemon wedges (optional)**
**Fresh dill sprigs (optional)**

Preheat oven to 375°F. Arrange salmon in large buttered baking dish; spread 2 tablespoons salad dressing over each steak. Sprinkle with chopped dill and parsley. Bake until fish flakes easily when tested with fork, 10 to 15 minutes. Place under broiler 45 to 60 seconds to brown. Serve with lemon wedges and garnish with dill sprigs, if desired.

*Makes 6 servings*

## SPICY HONEY GARLIC SHRIMP

**3 tablespoons vegetable oil**
**1 pound shrimp, peeled and deveined**
**½ teaspoon salt**
**5 tablespoons LEE KUM KEE® Honey Garlic Sauce**
**2 green onions, sliced**
**2 tablespoons LEE KUM KEE® Chili Garlic Sauce**

1. Heat oil in wok or skillet over medium heat.

2. Add shrimp and stir-fry until just pink. Sprinkle with salt while cooking.

3. Add honey garlic sauce, green onions and chili garlic sauce.

4. Stir-fry until green onions are tender and sauce is hot.

*Makes 4 servings*

# GRILLED GARLIC–PEPPER SHRIMP

**⅓ cup olive oil**
**2 tablespoons lemon juice**
**1 teaspoon garlic pepper blend**
**20 jumbo shrimp, peeled and deveined**
**Lemon wedges (optional)**

1. Prepare grill for direct grilling.

2. Meanwhile, combine oil, lemon juice and garlic pepper in large resealable plastic food storage bag; add shrimp. Marinate 30 minutes in refrigerator, turning bag once.

3. Thread 5 shrimp onto each of 4 skewers; reserve marinade. Grill on grid over medium heat 6 minutes or until pink and opaque, turning and brushing with marinade after 3 minutes. Serve with lemon wedges, if desired.

*Makes 4 servings*

# PASTA–SALMON SALAD

**8 ounces uncooked rotini pasta, cooked and drained**
**7 ounces canned salmon, drained**
**1 cup sliced celery**
**½ cup chopped green onions (optional)**
**⅔ cup flavored mayonnaise**

1. Combine pasta, salmon, celery and green onions, if desired in large bowl.

2. Add mayonnaise; toss until well coated.

*Makes 6 to 8 servings*

## Express Recipe

To make pan fried trout, lightly coat 4 pan-dressed trout with flour. Dip trout into 2 beaten eggs, then coat them with a mixture of ½ cup yellow cornmeal, 3 tablespoons all-purpose flour, 1 teaspoon salt and ¼ teaspoon black pepper. Pan fry fish in ½-inch of oil in a large skillet for 4 to 5 minutes per side until the fish flakes easily with a fork.

# GRILLED GLAZED SALMON

**⅓ cup apple juice**
**2 tablespoons soy sauce**
**½ teaspoon minced gingerroot**
**1¼ pounds salmon fillet**

1. Prepare grill for direct grilling. Combine apple juice, soy sauce, gingerroot and ⅛ teaspoon black pepper in small saucepan. Bring to a boil over medium heat. Reduce heat; simmer apple juice mixture about 10 minutes or until syrupy. Cool slightly.

2. Brush side of salmon fillet without skin with apple juice mixture. Grill salmon, flesh side down, on oiled grid over medium-hot heat 5 minutes. Turn and brush salmon with apple juice mixture. Grill 5 minutes more or until fish flakes easily with fork. *Makes 4 servings*

# ORIGINAL RANCH®
## FISH FILLETS

**1 packet (1 ounce) HIDDEN VALLEY® The Original Ranch® Salad Dressing & Seasoning Mix**
**1 package (19 ounces) breaded fish fillets or fish sticks**

Shake dressing mix and fillets in large plastic bag until coated. Bake at 400°F for 23 to 25 minutes. Serve with lemon wedges. *Makes 4 to 6 servings*

## Express Recipe

For a quick entrée, melt 2 tablespoons butter with 1 tablespoon vegetable oil in a medium skillet. Add 12 ounces of flour-coated sole fillets. Cook 2 minutes per side over medium heat until the fillets are golden brown and cooked through. Season with salt and black pepper. Serve fish with lemon wedges.

# One-Dish Meals

## VEGGIE SOUP

**1 bag (16 ounces) BIRDS EYE® frozen Mixed Vegetables**
**1 can (10¾ ounces) condensed tomato rice soup**
**1 can (10½ ounces) condensed French onion soup**
**1 soup can of water**

• In large saucepan, cook vegetables according to package directions; drain.

• Add both cans of soup and water; cook over medium-high heat until heated through.                    *Makes 4 servings*

SERVING SUGGESTION: Sprinkle individual servings evenly with 1 cup shredded Cheddar cheese.

**Prep Time:** 2 minutes
**Cook Time:** 10 to 12 minutes

## PASTA ALFREDO

**½ pound thin vegetable-flavored noodles, cooked and drained**
**½ cup grated Parmesan cheese**
**½ cup prepared HIDDEN VALLEY® The Original Ranch® Dressing**
**2 tablespoons chopped parsley**
**Additional Parmesan cheese and freshly ground black pepper, to taste**

In large pot, toss noodles, cheese, salad dressing and parsley. Warm over medium heat until cheese melts. Sprinkle individual servings with additional cheese and black pepper.

*Makes 4 servings*

## GROOVY ANGEL HAIR GOULASH

**1 pound lean ground beef**
**2 tablespoons margarine or butter**
**1 (4.8-ounce) package PASTA RONI® Angel Hair Pasta with Herbs**
**1 (14½-ounce) can diced tomatoes, undrained**
**1 cup frozen or canned corn, drained**

1. In large skillet over medium-high heat, brown ground beef. Remove from skillet; drain. Set aside.

2. In same skillet, bring 1½ cups water and margarine to a boil.

3. Stir in pasta; cook 1 minute or just until pasta softens slightly. Stir in tomatoes, corn, beef and Special Seasonings; return to a boil. Reduce heat to medium. Gently boil uncovered, 4 to 5 minutes or until pasta is tender, stirring frequently. Let stand 3 to 5 minutes before serving.

*Makes 4 servings*

**Prep Time:** 5 minutes
**Cook Time:** 15 minutes

## Express Recipe

On a cold wintry night serve Baked Potato Soup. Microwave 4 medium russet potatoes in a microwave-safe dish at HIGH power for 10 minutes or until tender; cool slightly. Sauté ½ cup sliced green onions in 2 tablespoons butter in large saucepan until tender. Stir in 2 tablespoons flour and ½ teaspoon salt; cook 1 minute. Stir in about 2 cups milk and coarsely mashed potatoes (remove and discard skins, if desired), stirring until the mixture comes to a boil. Remove from heat and stir in 1 cup shredded Cheddar cheese until melted. Serve with freshly ground black pepper.

## BEEFY BEAN & WALNUT STIR-FRY

**1 teaspoon vegetable oil**
**3 cloves garlic, minced**
**1 pound lean ground beef or ground turkey**
**1 bag (16 ounces) BIRDS EYE® frozen Cut Green Beans, thawed**
**1 teaspoon salt**
**½ cup walnut pieces**

• In large skillet, heat oil and garlic over medium heat about 30 seconds.

• Add beef and beans; sprinkle with salt. Mix well.

• Cook 5 minutes or until beef is well browned, stirring occasionally.

• Stir in walnuts; cook 2 minutes more.        *Makes 4 servings*

SERVING SUGGESTION: Serve over hot cooked egg noodles or rice.

**Prep Time:** 5 minutes
**Cook Time:** 7 to 10 minutes

## HAM & POTATO SOUP

**1 package (5 ounces) scalloped potatoes plus ingredients as package directs**
**1 bag (16 ounces) BIRDS EYE® frozen Broccoli Cuts**
**½ pound cooked ham, cut into ½-inch cubes**
**½ cup shredded Cheddar cheese (optional)**

• Prepare potatoes according to package directions for stove top method, adding broccoli and ham when adding milk and butter.

• Stir in cheese just before serving.        *Makes 4 servings*

SERVING SUGGESTION: Spoon mixture into shallow casserole dish. Sprinkle with cheese; broil until lightly browned.

**Prep Time:** 5 minutes
**Cook Time:** 25 minutes

---

## Express Recipe

To turn leftover chicken into a quick dinner for four, cook 8 ounces of rotini pasta according to package directions. Drain pasta. In the same saucepan cook and stir 1 diced red bell pepper in 1 tablespoon olive oil until it is tender. Stir in hot pasta and 1½ cups cubed or shredded cooked chicken and cook until the chicken is hot. Remove from heat and stir in ½ cup grated Parmesan cheese and black pepper to taste.

## RAINBOW SPIRALS

**4 (10-inch) flour tortillas (assorted flavors and colors)**
**4 tablespoons *French's*® Mustard (any flavor)**
**½ pound (about 8 slices) thinly sliced deli roast beef,**
**    bologna or turkey**
**8 slices American, provolone or Muenster cheese**
**    Fancy Party Toothpicks**

1. Spread each tortilla with *1 tablespoon* mustard. Layer with meat and cheeses dividing evenly.

2. Roll up jelly-roll style; secure with toothpicks and cut into thirds. Arrange on platter.              *Makes 4 to 6 servings*

**Prep Time:** 10 minutes

## RICE-STUFFED PEPPERS

**1 package LIPTON® Sides Rice & Sauce—Cheddar**
**    Broccoli**
**2 cups water**
**1 tablespoon I CAN'T BELIEVE IT'S NOT BUTTER!® Spread**
**1 pound ground beef**
**4 large red or green bell peppers, halved lengthwise**
**    and seeded**

Preheat oven to 350°F.

Prepare rice & sauce—cheddar broccoli with water and I Can't Believe It's Not Butter!® Spread according to package directions.

Meanwhile, in 10-inch skillet, brown ground beef over medium-high heat; drain. Stir into rice & sauce. Fill each pepper half with rice mixture. In 13×9-inch baking dish, arrange stuffed peppers. Bake covered 20 minutes. Remove cover and continue baking 10 minutes or until peppers are tender. Sprinkle, if desired, with shredded cheddar cheese.

*Makes about 4 main-dish servings*

## SHRIMP CREOLE STEW

1½ cups raw small shrimp, shelled
  1 bag (16 ounces) BIRDS EYE® frozen Farm Fresh
     Mixtures Broccoli, Cauliflower & Red Peppers
  1 can (14½ ounces) diced tomatoes
1½ teaspoons salt
  1 teaspoon hot pepper sauce
  1 teaspoon vegetable oil

• In large saucepan, combine all ingredients.

• Cover; bring to a boil. Reduce heat to medium-low; simmer 20 minutes or until shrimp turn opaque.

*Makes 4 servings*

SERVING SUGGESTION: Serve over Spanish or white rice and with additional hot pepper sauce for added zip.

**Prep Time:** 5 minutes
**Cook Time:** 20 minutes

## COUNTRY VEGETABLE SOUP

3 cans (13¾ ounces each) chicken broth
1 cup water
1 package (4½ ounces) creamy chicken, rice and
    sauce mix
½ teaspoon dried basil
1 bag (16 ounces) BIRDS EYE® frozen Farm Fresh
    Mixtures Broccoli, Green Beans, Pearl Onions and
    Red Peppers

• Bring broth, water, rice and sauce mix, and basil to a boil in large saucepan over high heat.

• Reduce heat to medium. Cook, uncovered, 7 minutes.

• Add vegetables; cook 6 to 7 minutes or until rice and vegetables are tender. *Makes 4 servings*

**Prep Time:** 5 minutes
**Cook Time:** 15 minutes

# SCALLOPED CHICKEN & PASTA

¼ cup margarine or butter, divided
1 package (6.2 ounces) PASTA RONI® Shells & White Cheddar
2 cups frozen mixed vegetables
⅔ cup milk
2 cups chopped cooked chicken or ham
¼ cup dry bread crumbs

1. Preheat oven to 450°F.

2. In 3-quart saucepan, combine 2¼ cups water and 2 tablespoons margarine. Bring just to a boil. Stir in pasta and frozen vegetables. Reduce heat to medium.

3. Boil, uncovered, stirring frequently, 12 to 14 minutes or until most of water is absorbed. Add Special Seasonings, milk and chicken. Continue cooking 3 minutes.

4. Meanwhile, melt remaining 2 tablespoons margarine in small saucepan; stir in bread crumbs.

5. Transfer pasta mixture to 8- or 9-inch glass baking dish. Sprinkle with bread crumbs. Bake 10 minutes or until bread crumbs are browned and edges are bubbly.

*Makes 4 servings*

# SPAM™ VEGETABLE HASH

½ cup chopped onion
2 tablespoons butter or margarine
2 cups frozen cubed hash brown potatoes, thawed
1 (12-ounce) can SPAM® Classic, cubed
1 (10-ounce) package frozen peas and carrots, thawed
½ teaspoon black pepper

In large skillet over medium-high heat, sauté onion in butter until tender. Stir in potatoes. Cook, stirring occasionally, until potatoes are lightly browned. Stir in SPAM®, peas and carrots, and pepper. Cook, stirring occasionally, until thoroughly heated.

*Makes 4 to 6 servings*

# VEGETABLE MACARONI & CHEESE

**1 box (14 ounces) macaroni and cheese**
**1 bag (16 ounces) BIRDS EYE® frozen Farm Fresh**
**Mixtures Broccoli, Cauliflower and Carrots***

*\*Or, substitute any other Birds Eye® frozen Farm Fresh Mixtures variety.*

• Cook macaroni and cheese according to package directions. Add vegetables during last 5 minutes of cooking time. Continue preparing recipe according to package directions.

*Makes about 4 servings*

**Cook Time:** 15 to 20 minutes

# SPANISH PORK CHOPS

**4 pork chops (about 1 pound)**
**1 (6.8-ounce) package RICE-A-RONI® Spanish Rice**
**2 tablespoons margarine or butter**
**1 (14½-ounce) can diced tomatoes, undrained**

1. In large skillet over medium-high heat, brown pork chops 3 minutes on each side; set aside.

2. In same skillet, sauté rice-vermicelli with margarine until vermicelli is golden brown.

3. Slowly stir in 2¼ cups water, tomatoes and Special Seasonings; bring to a boil. Reduce heat to low. Cover; simmer 10 minutes.

4. Add pork chops; return to a simmer. Cover; simmer 8 to 10 minutes or until rice is tender and pork chops are no longer pink inside.

*Makes 4 servings*

**Prep Time:** 5 minutes
**Cook Time:** 30 minutes

## Quick Tip

When you're preparing a pasta and vegetable dish, you can save preparation time by cooking the fresh or frozen vegetables with the pasta. Just be sure to use a large enough pan to accommodate both.

# CHEESY CHICKEN POT PIE

**1 pound boneless, skinless chicken breast halves, cut into ½-inch chunks**
**1 tablespoon all-purpose flour**
**1 jar (1 pound) RAGÚ® Cheese Creations!® Double Cheddar Sauce**
**1 bag (16 ounces) frozen mixed vegetables, thawed**
**1 prepared pastry for single-crust pie**

Preheat oven to 425°F. In 2-quart casserole, toss chicken with flour. Stir in Ragú Cheese Creations! Sauce and vegetables. Cover casserole with prepared pastry. Press pastry around edge of casserole to seal; trim excess pastry, then flute edges. Cover with aluminum foil and bake 20 minutes. Remove foil and continue baking 20 minutes or until crust is golden and chicken is thoroughly cooked. Let stand 5 minutes before serving.                        *Makes 6 servings*

# SPANISH SKILLET SUPPER

**1 tablespoon vegetable oil**
**1 pound boneless skinless chicken breasts, cut into 1-inch cubes**
**2 cups hot water**
**1 package (4.4 ounces) Spanish rice and sauce mix**
**2 cups BIRDS EYE® frozen Green Peas**
**   Crushed red pepper flakes**

• Heat oil in large skillet over medium-high heat. Add chicken; cook and stir until lightly browned, about 5 minutes.

• Add hot water, rice and sauce mix; bring to boil. Reduce heat to medium-low; simmer, uncovered, 5 minutes.

• Stir in green peas; increase heat to medium-high. Cover and cook 5 minutes or until peas and rice are tender.

• Sprinkle with red pepper flakes.      *Makes about 4 servings*

**Prep Time:** 5 minutes
**Cook Time:** 20 minutes

## Quick Tip

Cheesy Chicken Pot Pie is the perfect way to use leftover chicken. For a change of pace, you can substitute cooked pork roast, turkey breast or even roast beef for the chicken.

# ONE-DISH MEAL

**2 bags SUCCESS® Rice**
   **Vegetable cooking spray**
**1 cup cubed cooked turkey-ham\***
**1 cup (4 ounces) shredded low-fat Cheddar cheese**
**1 cup peas**

*\*Or, use cooked turkey, ham or turkey franks.*

**Microwave Directions**
Prepare rice according to package directions.

Spray 1-quart microwave-safe dish with cooking spray; set aside. Place rice in medium bowl. Add ham, cheese and peas; mix lightly. Spoon into prepared dish; smooth into even layer with spoon. Microwave on HIGH 1 minute; stir. Microwave 30 seconds or until thoroughly heated.      *Makes 4 servings*

CONVENTIONAL OVEN DIRECTIONS: Assemble casserole as directed. Spoon into ovenproof 1-quart baking dish sprayed with vegetable cooking spray. Bake at 350°F until thoroughly heated, about 15 to 20 minutes.

# SPICY SPINACH PIZZA

**1 (10-ounce) package frozen chopped spinach, thawed**
      **and squeezed dry**
**1 (4-ounce) package crumbled feta cheese**
**2 tablespoons TABASCO® brand Green Pepper Sauce**
**1 (8-ounce) package prepared pizza crusts (2 small**
      **pizzas)**

Preheat oven to 400°F. Combine spinach, feta cheese and TABASCO® Green Pepper Sauce in medium bowl. Spoon spinach mixture onto prepared pizza crusts. Place on cookie sheet. Bake 10 minutes or until pizza is heated through and crust is crisp.      *Makes 4 servings*

*Quick Tip*

Feta cheese, made from goat or cow's milk, is a traditional Greek cheese. Cured and stored in a brine, it contributes a rich, tangy flavor to salads, simple unsauced pasta and vegetable dishes, and vegetable pizzas.

ta

ent
mixing bowl
spoon
ave-proof

4 serving

package directions. Cut up
es with knife on cutting board.
o mixing bowl and add cheese,
eas. Stir to mix well. Pour mixture into
dish and smooth into an even layer
in microwave and heat on high 1
d 30 seconds longer or until
carefully remove dish
ually into 4

## HEARTY MINESTRONE SOUP

**2 cans (10¾ ounces each) condensed Italian
   tomato soup**
**3 cups water**
**3 cups cooked vegetables, such as zucchini, peas, corn
   or beans**
**2 cups cooked ditalini pasta**
**1⅓ cups *French's*® French Fried Onions**

Combine soup and water in large saucepan. Add vegetables
and pasta. Bring to a boil. Reduce heat. Cook until heated
through, stirring often.

Place French Fried Onions in microwavable dish. Microwave
on HIGH 1 minute or until onions are golden.

Ladle soup into individual bowls. Sprinkle with French Fried
Onions.                                            *Makes 6 servings*

**Prep Time:** 10 minutes
**Cook Time:** 5 minutes

## CREAMY GARLIC CLAM SAUCE
## WITH LINGUINE

**1 jar (1 pound) RAGÚ® Cheese Creations!® Roasted Garlic
   Parmesan Sauce**
**2 cans (6½ ounces each) chopped clams, undrained**
**1 tablespoon chopped fresh parsley *or* ½ teaspoon
   dried parsley flakes**
**8 ounces linguine or spaghetti, cooked and drained**

1. In 3-quart saucepan, cook Ragú Cheese Creations! Sauce,
clams and parsley over medium heat, stirring occasionally,
10 minutes.

2. Serve over hot linguine and garnish, if desired, with fresh
lemon wedges.                                      *Makes 4 servings*

**Prep Time:** 5 minutes
**Cook Time:** 15 minutes

*Quick Tip*

Couscous is coarsely ground durum wheat. In the United States, most couscous is precooked which makes it a great quick-cooking product to keep in your pantry to help create spur-of-the-moment meals.

## CURRIED CHICKEN WITH COUSCOUS

**1 package (5.7 ounces) curry flavor couscous mix**
**1 tablespoon butter or margarine**
**1 pound boneless skinless chicken breasts, cut into thin strips**
**½ bag (16 ounces) BIRDS EYE® frozen Farm Fresh Mixtures Broccoli, Cauliflower & Red Peppers**
**1⅓ cups water**
**½ cup raisins**

• Remove seasoning packet from couscous mix; set aside.

• In large nonstick skillet, melt butter over medium-high heat. Add chicken; cook until browned on all sides.

• Stir in vegetables, water, raisins and seasoning packet; bring to boil. Reduce heat to medium-low; cover and simmer 5 minutes or until chicken is no longer pink in center.

• Stir in couscous; cover. Remove from heat; let stand 5 minutes. Stir before serving. Garnish as desired.

*Makes 4 servings*

BIRDS EYE IDEA: To add flavor to chicken breasts, simply rub them with lemon juice before cooking.

**Prep Time:** 5 minutes
**Cook Time:** 15 minutes

## CHILI STEW

**1 box (10 ounces) BIRDS EYE® frozen Sweet Corn**
**2 cans (15 ounces each) chili**
**1 can (14 ounces) stewed tomatoes**
**Chili powder**

• In large saucepan, cook corn according to package directions; drain.

• Stir in chili and tomatoes; cook until heated through.

• Stir in chili powder to taste.

*Makes 4 servings*

SERVING SUGGESTION: Serve with your favorite corn bread or sprinkle with shredded Cheddar cheese.

**Prep Time:** 2 minutes
**Cook Time:** 7 to 10 minutes

# SEAFOOD RISOTTO

**1 package (5.2 ounces) rice in creamy sauce (Risotto Milanese flavor)**
**1 package (14 to 16 ounces) frozen fully cooked shrimp**
**1 box (10 ounces) BIRDS EYE® frozen Mixed Vegetables**
**2 teaspoons grated Parmesan cheese**

• In 4-quart saucepan, prepare rice according to package directions. Add frozen shrimp and vegetables during last 10 minutes of cooking.

• Sprinkle with cheese.                    *Makes 4 servings*

SERVING SUGGESTION: Serve with garlic bread and a tossed green salad.

**Prep Time:** 5 minutes
**Cook Time:** 15 minutes

# FRENCH–AMERICAN RICE

**½ pound lean ground beef or ground turkey**
**1 box (10 ounces) BIRDS EYE® frozen White and Wild Rice**
**½ cup California walnuts**
**1½ teaspoons soy sauce**

• In large skillet, cook beef over medium-high heat 5 minutes or until well browned.

• Stir in rice; cook 5 minutes more or until rice is tender, stirring occasionally.

• Stir in California walnuts and soy sauce; cook 1 minute or until heated.                    *Makes 4 servings*

**Prep Time:** 5 minutes
**Cook Time:** 10 minutes

---

*Express Recipe*

Take advantage of the convenience of macaroni and cheese mixes by simply adding additional ingredients. Prepare macaroni and cheese following the package directions. Stir in ½ cup crisply cooked and crumbled bacon (10 slices) or real bacon pieces and 2 small tomatoes, cut into small pieces. Makes 3 servings.

## *Express Recipe*

For a last-minute chili for 3, combine 1 (15-ounce) can drained kidney beans, 1 (15-ounce) can mild or hot chili beans and 1 (14-ounce) can diced tomatoes with green chilies in a medium saucepan. Simmer 15 minutes, then add 6 ounces of cubed smoked fully-cooked sausage. Simmer until the sausage is hot. Top with chopped green onion and shredded Monterey Jack cheese, if desired.

## VEGETABLE PIZZA

**2 to 3 cups BIRDS EYE® frozen Farm Fresh Mixtures
Broccoli, Red Peppers, Onions and Mushrooms
1 Italian bread shell or pizza crust, about 12 inches
1 to 1½ cups shredded mozzarella cheese
Dried oregano, basil or Italian seasoning**

• Preheat oven according to directions on pizza crust package.

• Rinse vegetables in colander under warm water. Drain well; pat with paper towel to remove excess moisture.

• Spread crust with half the cheese and all the vegetables. Sprinkle with herbs; top with remaining cheese.

• Follow baking directions on pizza crust package; bake until hot and bubbly.                              *Makes 3 to 4 servings*

**Prep Time:** 5 minutes
**Cook Time:** 15 minutes

## BROCCOLI CHICKEN AU GRATIN

**1 (6.5-ounce) package RICE-A-RONI® Broccoli Au Gratin
2½ tablespoons margarine or butter
¾ pound boneless, skinless chicken breasts, cut into
     thin strips
2 cups frozen chopped broccoli
1 cup fresh sliced mushrooms
¼ teaspoon coarse ground black pepper**

1. In large skillet over medium heat, sauté rice-pasta mix with margarine until pasta is light golden brown.

2. Slowly stir in 2¼ cups water, chicken and Special Seasonings; bring to a boil. Reduce heat to low. Cover; simmer 10 minutes.

3. Stir in broccoli, mushrooms and pepper. Cover; cook 5 to 10 minutes or until rice is tender and chicken is no longer pink. Let stand 3 to 5 minutes before serving.
                                                   *Makes 4 servings*

**Prep Time:** 5 minutes
**Cook Time:** 30 minutes

# ASIAN CHICKEN AND NOODLES

**1 package (3 ounces) chicken flavor instant ramen
   noodles
1 bag (16 ounces) BIRDS EYE® frozen Farm Fresh
   Mixtures Broccoli, Carrots and Water Chestnuts\***
**1 tablespoon vegetable oil
1 pound boneless skinless chicken breasts, cut into
   thin strips
¼ cup stir-fry sauce**

*\*Or, substitute 1 bag (16 ounces) Birds Eye® frozen Broccoli Cuts.*

• Reserve seasoning packet from noodles.

• Bring 2 cups water to a boil in large saucepan. Add noodles
and vegetables. Cook 3 minutes, stirring occasionally; drain.

• Meanwhile, heat oil in large nonstick skillet over medium-
high heat. Add chicken; cook and stir until browned, about
8 minutes.

• Stir in noodles, vegetables, stir-fry sauce and reserved
seasoning packet; heat through.        *Makes about 4 servings*

**Prep Time:** 5 minutes
**Cook Time:** 20 minutes

# ITALIAN SAUSAGE SOUP

**2 boxes (10 ounces each) BIRDS EYE® frozen Italian Style
   Vegetables & Bow-Tie Pasta
2 cans (14 ounces each) beef broth
1 pound cooked Italian sausage, cubed
1 can (8 ounces) tomato sauce**

• In large saucepan, place vegetables and broth; bring to boil
over high heat. Reduce heat to medium; cover and simmer
7 to 10 minutes or until vegetables are crisp-tender.

• Stir in cooked sausage and tomato sauce; cook until heated
through.                                *Makes 4 servings*

**Prep Time:** 2 minutes
**Cook Time:** 10 to 12 minutes

# VEGETABLE FRITTATA

**2 tablespoons butter or margarine**
**1 bag (16 ounces) BIRDS EYE® frozen Farm Fresh**
**Mixtures Broccoli, Corn and Red Peppers**
**8 eggs**
**½ cup water**
**1 tablespoon TABASCO® Pepper Sauce**
**¾ teaspoon salt**

• Melt butter in 12-inch nonstick skillet over medium heat. Add vegetables; cook and stir 3 minutes.

• Lightly beat eggs, water, Tabasco sauce and salt.

• Pour egg mixture over vegetables in skillet. Cover and cook 10 to 15 minutes or until eggs are set.

• To serve, cut into wedges.          *Makes about 4 servings*

SERVING SUGGESTION: Serve with warm crusty bread and a green salad.

**Prep Time:** 5 minutes
**Cook Time:** 20 minutes

# RIGATONI WITH BABY CLAMS AND SAUSAGE

**1 package (16 ounces) uncooked BARILLA® rigatoni**
**2 tablespoons olive oil**
**1 pound Italian sausage, cut into ¼-inch-thick slices**
**1 can (10 ounces) baby clams, drained**
**1 jar (26 ounces) BARILLA® Roasted Garlic & Onion Sauce**
**Chopped parsley and grated Parmesan cheese for garnish**

Prepare rigatoni according to package directions; drain.

Heat oil in large skillet over medium heat. Add sausage; cook and stir 10 minutes or until no longer pink. Add clams and BARILLA® sauce; cook until heated through.

Add sauce mixture to cooked rigatoni in large bowl and toss well. Garnish with parsley and Parmesan, if desired. Serve immediately.          *Makes 4 to 6 servings*

# SOUTHWESTERN SOUP

**1 bag (16 ounces) BIRDS EYE® frozen Corn**
**2 cans (15 ounces each) chili**
**1 cup hot water**
**½ cup chopped green bell pepper**

• Combine all ingredients in saucepan.

• Cook over medium heat 10 to 12 minutes.

*Makes 4 to 6 servings*

**Prep Time:** 1 to 2 minutes
**Cook Time:** 10 to 12 minutes

# HERBED CHICKEN AND POTATOES

**2 medium all-purpose potatoes, thinly sliced (about**
**1 pound)**
**4 bone-in chicken breast halves (about 2 pounds)\***
**1 envelope LIPTON® RECIPE SECRETS® Savory Herb with**
**Garlic Soup Mix**
**⅓ cup water**
**1 tablespoon BERTOLLI® Olive Oil**

*\*Substitution: Use 1 (2½- to 3-pound) chicken, cut into serving pieces.*

1. Preheat oven to 425°F. In 13×9-inch baking or roasting pan, add potatoes; arrange chicken over potatoes.

2. Pour soup mix blended with water and oil over chicken and potatoes.

3. Bake uncovered 40 minutes or until chicken is thoroughly cooked and potatoes are tender.
*Makes 4 servings*

## CHICKEN AND ASPARAGUS HOLLANDAISE

**1 package (1.25 ounces) hollandaise sauce mix**
**1 pound boneless skinless chicken breasts, cut into strips**
**2 teaspoons lemon juice**
**1 box (10 ounces) BIRDS EYE® frozen Asparagus**
**Dash cayenne pepper (optional)**

• Prepare hollandaise sauce according to package directions.

• Spray large skillet with nonstick cooking spray; cook chicken strips over medium-high heat 10 to 12 minutes or until browned, stirring occasionally.

• Add hollandaise sauce, lemon juice and asparagus.

• Cover and cook, stirring occasionally, 5 to 10 minutes or until asparagus is heated through. *Do not overcook.*

• Add cayenne pepper, salt and black pepper to taste.

*Makes 4 to 6 servings*

SERVING SUGGESTION: Serve over rice or noodles.

**Prep Time:** 10 minutes
**Cook Time:** 20 to 25 minutes

## SKILLET PASTA DINNER

**1 pound ground beef**
**1 jar (1 pound 10 ounces) RAGÚ® Robusto! Pasta Sauce**
**8 ounces rotini pasta, cooked and drained**
**1 cup shredded cheddar or Monterey Jack cheese, divided**
**2 teaspoons chili powder (optional)**

In 12-inch skillet, brown ground beef over medium-high heat; drain. Stir in Ragú Robusto! Pasta Sauce, hot pasta, ¾ cup cheese and chili powder. Simmer uncovered, stirring occasionally, 5 minutes or until heated through. Sprinkle with remaining ¼ cup cheese.

*Makes 4 servings*

---

## Express Recipe

Take 10 minutes to prepare a quiche for baking, then while it bakes spend time with your family. In a large bowl, beat 4 eggs. Stir in 1½ cups of milk or half-and-half, 2 cups shredded Cheddar cheese, 1 cup cooked broccoli florets, ¼ teaspoon salt and ⅛ teaspoon black pepper. Pour into a 9-inch unbaked pie shell. Bake in a preheated 350°F oven for 50 to 55 minutes. Cool 15 minutes and serve.

## GARLIC HERB CHICKEN AND RICE SKILLET

**4 boneless, skinless chicken breasts (about 1 pound)**
**1¾ cups water**
**1 box UNCLE BEN'S® COUNTRY INN® Chicken Flavored Rice**
**2 cups frozen broccoli, carrots and cauliflower**
**¼ cup garlic and herb flavored soft spreadable cheese**

1. In large skillet, combine chicken, water and contents of seasoning packet. Bring to a boil. Reduce heat; cover and simmer 10 minutes.

2. Add rice, vegetables and cheese. Cook covered 10 to 15 minutes or until chicken is no longer pink in center. Remove from heat; let stand 5 minutes or until liquid is absorbed. *Makes 4 servings*

## SWEET & SOUR STIR-FRY

**1 tablespoon vegetable oil**
**½ pound boneless chicken breast or beef, cut into thin strips**
**1 bag (16 ounces) BIRDS EYE® frozen Farm Fresh Mixtures Sugar Snap Stir-Fry**
**1 tablespoon water**
**½ cup prepared sweet & sour sauce**

• Heat oil in large skillet or wok. Stir-fry chicken until cooked through.

• Add vegetables and water; cover and cook 5 to 7 minutes over medium-high heat.

• Stir in sweet & sour sauce; heat through.

• Serve hot over rice or pasta. *Makes 3 to 4 servings*

**Prep Time:** 5 minutes
**Cook Time:** 12 to 15 minutes

---

### Express Recipe

To make Chicken Barley Soup for two, brown 1 diced chicken breast in 1 tablespoon oil in a 2-quart saucepan. Add 1 cup sliced mushrooms, ½ cup chopped carrot and ¼ cup sliced green onions; cook and stir until vegetables are tender. Add 2½ cups chicken broth, ⅓ cup quick-cooking barley and ¼ teaspoon salt. Bring to a boil. Simmer, covered, 15 to 20 minutes or until the barley is tender. Season to taste with salt pepper.

## TURKEY & RICE BUNDLES

**1 package LIPTON® Sides Rice & Sauce—Chicken Broccoli**
**2 cups water**
**4 turkey cutlets (about 1 pound), pounded thin**
**1 jar (7 ounces) roasted red peppers, drained**
**¼ cup water**

Preheat oven to 350°F.

In medium saucepan, bring rice & sauce—chicken broccoli and 2 cups water to a boil. Reduce heat and simmer uncovered, stirring occasionally, 10 minutes; set aside.

Evenly top each cutlet with roasted peppers, then spread with ¼ cup rice mixture; bring up sides to form bundles and secure with wooden toothpicks.

In 11×7-inch baking dish, combine remaining rice mixture with ¼ cup water. Arrange turkey bundles over rice. Bake 25 minutes or until turkey is done.     *Makes 4 servings*

VARIATION: Use 4 boneless, skinless chicken breast halves (about 1 pound), pounded thin.

## BELGIOIOSO® MOZZARELLA PIZZA

**2 (13-inch) refrigerated pizza crusts**
**3 tablespoons olive oil, divided**
**4 ripe plum tomatoes, cut into thin slices**
**2 cups diced BELGIOIOSO® Fresh Mozzarella Cheese**
**12 fresh basil leaves**
**½ teaspoon salt**

Preheat oven to 425°F. Place pizza crusts on lightly oiled pans. Brush each with 1 tablespoon olive oil. Place tomato slices on crusts; layer with BelGioioso Fresh Mozzarella Cheese and basil leaves. Sprinkle with salt and remaining 1 tablespoon olive oil. Bake pizzas 25 to 30 minutes or until top and bottom crusts are nicely browned. Cut into wedges and serve.     *Makes 2 pizzas*

## CHICKEN GUMBO

**3 tablespoons vegetable oil**
**1 pound boneless skinless chicken breasts, cut into**
    **1-inch pieces**
**½ pound smoked sausage,\* cut into ¾-inch slices**
**1 bag (16 ounces) BIRDS EYE® frozen Farm Fresh**
    **Mixtures Broccoli, Corn and Red Peppers**
**1 can (14½ ounces) stewed tomatoes**
**1½ cups water**

*\*For a spicy gumbo, use andouille sausage. Any type of kielbasa or turkey kielbasa can also be used.*

• Heat oil in large saucepan over high heat. Add chicken and sausage; cook until browned, about 8 minutes.

• Add vegetables, tomatoes and water; bring to boil. Reduce heat to medium; cover and cook 5 to 6 minutes.

*Makes 4 to 6 servings*

**Prep Time:** 5 minutes
**Cook Time:** 20 minutes

## CHICKEN TIKKA MASALA

**2 tablespoons vegetable oil**
**1 pound boneless skinless chicken breast, cubed**
**1 (15-ounce) jar PATAK'S® Tikka Masala Cooking Sauce**
  **Hot cooked rice**

In large skillet over medium-high heat, heat oil. Add chicken and sauté 2 minutes. Add cooking sauce and stir well. Reduce heat, cover and simmer 25 to 30 minutes, stirring occasionally, or until chicken is cooked through. Serve over hot cooked rice.

*Makes 4 servings*

# CAJUN CHICKEN BAYOU

**2 cups water**
**1 can (10 ounces) diced tomatoes and green chilies, undrained**
**1 box UNCLE BEN'S CHEF'S RECIPE® Traditional Red Beans & Rice**
**2 boneless, skinless chicken breasts (about 8 ounces)**

1. In large skillet, combine water, tomatoes, beans & rice and contents of seasoning packet; mix well.

2. Add chicken. Bring to a boil. Cover; reduce heat and simmer 20 minutes or until chicken is no longer pink in center.                                    *Makes 2 servings*

TIP: If you prefer a spicier dish, add hot pepper sauce just before serving.

# CHICKEN DI NAPOLITANO

**1 tablespoon olive oil**
**2 boneless, skinless chicken breasts (about 8 ounces)**
**1 can (14½ ounces) diced tomatoes, undrained**
**1¼ cups water**
**1 box UNCLE BEN'S® COUNTRY INN® Rice Pilaf**
**¼ cup chopped fresh basil *or* 1½ teaspoons dried basil leaves**

1. Heat oil in large skillet. Add chicken; cook over medium-high heat 8 to 10 minutes or until lightly browned on both sides.

2. Add tomatoes, water, rice and contents of seasoning packet. Bring to a boil. Cover; reduce heat and simmer 15 to 18 minutes or until chicken is no longer pink in center and liquid is absorbed.

3. Stir in basil. Slice chicken and serve over rice.
*Makes 2 servings*

TIP: For more flavor, substitute diced tomatoes with Italian herbs or roasted garlic for diced tomatoes.

*Quick Tip*

Flavored canned tomato products are convenient pantry staples. Keep diced tomatoes with green chilies, Italian seasonings or roasted garlic on hand for a quick burst of flavor in skillet dishes and casseroles.

## PEPPERS PENNE

**8 ounces BARILLA® Penne or Mostaccioli**
**1 tablespoon olive or vegetable oil**
**1 each red, green and yellow bell pepper, cut into long, thin strips**
**1 jar (26 ounces) BARILLA® Marinara Pasta Sauce**
**2 tablespoons grated Parmesan cheese**

1. Cook penne according to package directions; drain.

2. Meanwhile, heat olive oil in large skillet. Add bell peppers; cook and stir over high heat 1 minute. Reduce heat; stir in pasta sauce. Cook 5 minutes over medium heat, stirring frequently.

3. Pour pepper mixture over hot drained penne. Sprinkle with cheese.                    *Makes 6 to 8 servings*

VARIATION: Add 1 cup coarsely chopped pepperoni with the pasta sauce.

## SPICY SAUSAGE AND ROASTED GARLIC SAUCE FOR SPAGHETTI

**1 package (16 ounces) BARILLA® Thin Spaghetti**
**1 tablespoon olive or vegetable oil**
**1 pound bulk hot Italian sausage**
**2 jars (26 ounces each) BARILLA® Roasted Garlic and Onion Pasta Sauce**

1. Cook spaghetti according to package directions; drain.

2. Meanwhile, heat oil in large nonstick skillet over medium heat. Add sausage; cook 5 to 6 minutes or until brown, stirring to break up sausage. Drain off excess fat from skillet.

3. Add pasta sauce to skillet. Reduce heat; cook and stir 10 minutes. Combine hot drained spaghetti with sauce mixture.                    *Makes 8 servings*

---

## Express Recipe

In 30 minutes you can make a delicious bacon and potato frittata. Simply melt 2 tablespoons butter in a large (10-inch) skillet over medium heat. Add 2 cups refrigerated shredded hash brown potatoes. Cook 3 minutes, stirring frequently. Beat 5 eggs in a medium bowl and stir in $^1/_2$ cup crisply cooked and crumbled bacon, $^1/_4$ cup half-and-half, $^1/_8$ teaspoon *each* salt and black pepper. Pour this mixture over the hash browns and cover the skillet. Cook about 6 to 7 minutes or until the egg mixture is set. Cut into 4 wedges.

## Express Recipe

Cook up a quick meal with just four ingredients. Cook 8 ounces of linguine according to package directions, adding 1⅓ cups of green beans cut into 1½ inch pieces during the last 6 minutes of cooking. Drain and place in a large bowl. Heat one 16-ounce jar Alfredo or Parmesan sauce in the same saucepan and pour over the pasta mixture. Toss until well blended.

# TRADITIONAL BROCCOLI STIR-FRY

**2 tablespoons oil**
**½ pound beef, thinly sliced**
**1 bag (16 ounces) BIRDS EYE® frozen Farm Fresh Mixtures Broccoli Stir-Fry**
**1 tablespoon water**
**½ cup prepared stir-fry sauce\***

*\*Or, substitute 1 package stir-fry seasoning mix, prepared according to package directions.*

• Heat oil in large skillet. Add beef; cook and stir over medium heat 6 to 7 minutes.

• Add vegetables and water; cover and cook 5 to 7 minutes.

• Add stir-fry sauce; cook, uncovered, until heated through.

*Makes 2 to 4 servings*

SERVING SUGGESTION: Serve over rice.

**Prep Time:** 5 minutes
**Cook Time:** 12 to 15 minutes

# BARBECUE PORK ON BUNS

**1 (2-pound) boneless pork loin**
**1 onion, chopped**
**¾ cup cola-flavored carbonated beverage**
**¾ cup barbecue sauce**
**8 sandwich buns**

### Slow Cooker Directions

Combine all ingredients except buns in a 4-quart slow cooker; cook, covered, on HIGH for 5 to 6 hours or until very tender. Drain; slice or shred pork. Serve on buns with additional barbecue sauce, if desired.     *Makes 8 servings*

TIP: Pork can be made 1 to 2 days ahead; refrigerate covered and reheat before serving.

*Favorite recipe from **National Pork Board***

## VEGGIE TUNA PASTA

**1 package (16 ounces) medium pasta shells**
**1 bag (16 ounces) BIRDS EYE® frozen Farm Fresh**
**Mixtures Broccoli, Corn & Red Peppers**
**1 can (10 ounces) chunky light tuna, packed in water**
**1 can (10¾ ounces) reduced-fat cream of mushroom soup**

• In large saucepan, cook pasta according to package directions. Add vegetables during last 10 minutes; drain and return to saucepan.

• Stir in tuna and soup. Add salt and pepper to taste. Cook over medium heat until heated through.    *Makes 4 servings*

VARIATION: Stir in 1 can (4 to 6 ounces) chopped ripe olives with tuna.

SERVING SUGGESTION: For a creamier dish, add a few tablespoons water with soup; blend well.

BIRDS EYE IDEA: Be prepared for unexpected company by stocking your freezer with your favorite Birds Eye® Easy Recipe entrées and chicken breasts.

**Prep Time:** 2 minutes
**Cook Time:** 12 to 15 minutes

## BLACK BEAN SOUP

**¼ cup mild salsa**
**1 can (16 ounces) black beans**
**2 cups water**
**1 cup cherry tomatoes, tops removed**
**1½ teaspoons cumin**
**1 teaspoon sugar**

Strain salsa, discarding chunks. Drain and rinse black beans; reserve 1 tablespoon. Place remaining beans with all ingredients in food processor or blender; process until smooth. Stir in reserved black beans and refrigerate until ready to serve.    *Makes 4 servings*

*Favorite recipe from **The Sugar Association, Inc.***

# Snappy Side Dishes

To add a delicious spark to broccoli, toss warm cooked broccoli florets and 2 tablespoons toasted pine nuts with a well-blended mixture of 2 tablespoons olive oil, 1 tablespoon lemon juice, ¼ teaspoon *each* of salt and dry mustard, and black pepper to taste.

## ORIGINAL RANCH® ROASTED POTATOES

**2 pounds small red potatoes, quartered**
**¼ cup vegetable oil**
**1 packet (1 ounce) HIDDEN VALLEY® The Original Ranch®**
**Salad Dressing & Seasoning Mix**

Place potatoes in a gallon-size Glad® Zipper Storage Bag. Pour oil over potatoes. Seal bag and toss to coat. Add salad dressing & seasoning mix; seal bag and toss again until coated. Bake in ungreased baking pan at 450°F for 30 to 35 minutes or until potatoes are brown and crisp.

*Makes 4 to 6 servings*

## APRICOT RICE

**2½ cups water**
**¼ cup finely chopped dried apricots**
**¼ teaspoon salt**
**1 cup long-grain rice**

1. Combine water, apricots and salt in medium saucepan. Bring to a boil; stir in rice.

2. Cover; reduce heat and simmer 20 minutes. Remove from heat; let stand 5 minutes. *Makes 3 cups rice*

## SAUTÉED SNOW PEAS & BABY CARROTS

**1 tablespoon I CAN'T BELIEVE IT'S NOT BUTTER!® Spread**
**2 tablespoons chopped shallots or onion**
**5 ounces frozen whole baby carrots, partially thawed**
**4 ounces snow peas (about 1 cup)**
**2 teaspoons chopped fresh parsley (optional)**

In 12-inch nonstick skillet, melt I Can't Believe It's Not Butter!® Spread over medium heat and cook shallots, stirring occasionally, 1 minute or until almost tender. Add carrots and snow peas and cook, stirring occasionally, 4 minutes or until crisp-tender. Stir in parsley and heat through.

*Makes 2 servings*

NOTE: Recipe can be doubled.

## MASHED ONION-ROASTED POTATOES

**1 envelope LIPTON® RECIPE SECRETS® Onion Soup Mix***
**4 medium all-purpose potatoes, cut into large chunks (about 2 pounds)**
**⅓ cup BERTOLLI® Olive Oil**
**1¾ cups hot milk**

*\*Also terrific with LIPTON® RECIPE SECRETS® Savory Herb with Garlic Soup Mix.*

1. Preheat oven to 450°F. In large plastic bag or bowl, add all ingredients except milk. Close bag and shake, or toss in bowl, until potatoes are evenly coated.

2. In 13×9-inch baking or roasting pan, arrange potatoes; discard bag.

3. Bake uncovered, stirring occasionally, 40 minutes or until potatoes are tender and golden brown.

4. Turn potatoes into large bowl. Mash potatoes; stir in hot milk.

*Makes 4 servings*

*Quick Tip*

To peel or not to peel, that is the question. When making mashed potatoes, leave the skins on because they provide extra nutrients and a wonderful flavor. Best of all, you'll spend less time in the kitchen.

## GREEN BEANS WITH PINE NUTS

**1 pound green beans, trimmed**
**2 tablespoons butter or margarine**
**2 tablespoons pine nuts**

Cook beans in 1 inch water in covered 3-quart saucepan 6 to 8 minutes or until beans are crisp-tender; drain. Melt butter in large skillet over medium heat. Add pine nuts; cook, stirring frequently, until golden. Add beans; stir gently to coat beans with butter. Season with salt and pepper to taste.

*Makes 4 servings*

## FRESH CORN WITH ADOBE BUTTER

**½ teaspoon chili powder**
**1 teaspoon lime juice**
**¼ cup butter or margarine, softened**
**4 ears yellow or white corn, husks and silk removed**

Moisten chili powder with lime juice in small bowl. Add butter; stir until well blended. Season to taste with salt. Place in small crock or bowl. Place corn in 5-quart pan; cover with cold water. Cover pan and bring to a boil. Boil 1 minute. Turn off heat; let stand 2 minutes or until corn is tender. Drain. Serve with butter mixture.

*Makes 4 servings*

## MEXICAN REFRIED BEANS

**1 can (1 pound 14 ounces) refried beans**
**1 package (1.0 ounce) LAWRY'S® Taco Spices & Seasonings**
**2 cups (8 ounces) shredded cheddar cheese**
**¼ cup finely chopped onion**

In 2½-quart casserole dish, combine all ingredients. Cover and bake in 350°F oven for 20 to 25 minutes.

*Makes about 4 cups (6 to 8 servings)*

SERVING SUGGESTION: Serve with your favorite Mexican foods—tacos, burritos, flautas and enchiladas!

**Prep Time:** 10 minutes
**Cook Time:** 20 to 25 minutes

---

*Express Recipe*

To make an easy but special rice dish, simply prepare rice according to package directions but substitute chicken broth for the water. When the rice is tender and all the broth has been absorbed, stir in ¼ cup toasted slivered almonds, ¼ cup finely chopped green onions and 1 tablespoon butter.

## BERRY FILLED MUFFINS

**1 package DUNCAN HINES® Bakery-Style Wild Maine Blueberry Muffin Mix**
**1 egg**
**½ cup water**
**¼ cup strawberry jam**
**2 tablespoons sliced natural almonds**

1. Preheat oven to 400°F. Place 8 (2½-inch) paper or foil liners in muffin cups; set aside.

2. Rinse blueberries from Mix with cold water and drain.

3. Empty muffin mix into bowl. Break up any lumps. Add egg and water. Stir until moistened, about 50 strokes. Fill cups half full with batter.

4. Fold blueberries into jam. Spoon on top of batter in each cup. Spread gently. Cover with remaining batter. Sprinkle with almonds. Bake at 400°F for 17 to 20 minutes or until set and golden brown. Cool in pan 5 to 10 minutes. Loosen carefully before removing from pan.          *Makes 8 muffins*

TIP: For a delicious flavor variation, try using blackberry or red raspberry jam instead of the strawberry jam.

## CHEDDAR BROCCOLI POTATOES

**6 hot baked potatoes, split open lengthwise**
**1½ cups chopped cooked broccoli**
**1⅓ cups *French's*® French Fried Onions**
**¾ cup pasteurized process American cheese sauce, melted**

1. Place potatoes on microwave-safe dish. Scrape cooked potato with fork to fluff up. Top with broccoli and French Fried Onions, dividing evenly.

2. Microwave on HIGH 2 minutes or until onions are golden.

3. Drizzle melted cheese sauce on top.          *Makes 6 servings*

**Prep Time:** 20 minutes
**Cook Time:** 2 minutes

# Express Recipe

Corn muffins are a great edition to many dinner menus. Save time by starting with a mix. To make corn muffins more distinctive, prepare a 7-ounce mix according to package directions, then stir ⅓ cup real bacon bits or crisply cooked and crumbled bacon and 1 (4-ounce) can drained, diced mild green chilies into the batter. Bake as directed on the package.

## LOW-FAT CAJUN WEDGES

**4 russet potatoes**
**Nonstick cooking spray**
**1 tablespoons cajun seasoning or other seasoning, such as paprika**
**Purple kale and fresh sage leaves, for garnish**

1. Preheat oven to 400°F. To prepare potatoes, scrub under running water with soft vegetable brush; rinse. Dry well. (Do not peel.) Line baking sheet with foil and spray with cooking spray.

2. Cut potatoes in half lengthwise; then cut each half lengthwise into 3 wedges. Place potatoes, skin side down, in single layer on prepared baking sheet.

3. Spray potatoes lightly with cooking spray and sprinkle with seasoning.

4. Bake 25 minutes or until browned and fork-tender. Garnish, if desired. Serve immediately.    *Makes 4 servings*

LOW-FAT POTATO CHIPS: Follow step 1 as directed. Slice potatoes crosswise as thin as possible with chef's knife or mandoline slicer. Place in single layer on prepared baking sheet; spray and season as directed. Bake 10 to 15 minutes or until browned and crisp. Serve immediately.

LOW-FAT COTTAGE FRIES: Follow step 1 as directed. Cut potatoes crosswise into ¼-inch-thick slices. Place in single layer on prepared baking sheet; spray and season as directed. Bake 15 to 20 minutes or until browned and fork-tender. Serve immediately.

## SAUCY VEGETABLE CASSEROLE

**2 bags (16 ounces each) frozen mixed vegetables (broccoli, cauliflower, carrots), thawed**
**2 cups *French's*® French Fried Onions, divided**
**1 package (16 ounces) pasteurized process cheese, cut into ¼-inch slices**

1. Preheat oven to 350°F. Combine vegetables and *1 cup* French Fried Onions in shallow 3-quart baking dish. Top evenly with cheese slices.

2. Bake 15 minutes or until hot and cheese is almost melted; stir. Top with remaining onions and bake 5 minutes or until onions are golden.                    *Makes 8 servings*

VARIATION: For added Cheddar flavor, substitute *French's*® **Cheddar French Fried Onions** for the original flavor.

**Prep Time:** 5 minutes
**Cook Time:** 20 minutes

## DOUBLE CHEDDAR BACON MASHED POTATOES

**2 pounds all-purpose potatoes, peeled and sliced**
**1 jar (1 pound) RAGÚ® Cheese Creations!® Double Cheddar Sauce, heated**
**5 slices bacon, crisp-cooked and crumbled (about ¼ cup)**
**1 teaspoon salt**

1. In 3-quart saucepan, cover potatoes with water. Bring to a boil over high heat. Reduce heat to low and simmer uncovered 15 minutes or until potatoes are very tender; drain. Return potatoes to saucepan. Mash potatoes.

2. Stir Ragú Cheese Creations! Sauce into mashed potatoes. Stir in bacon and salt.                    *Makes 6 servings*

TIP: Stir in ¼ cup chopped green onions for an extra flavor boost.

**Prep Time:** 10 minutes
**Cook Time:** 20 minutes

## GREEN BEAN SALAD

**1 pound fresh green beans, trimmed**
**3 tablespoons lemon juice**
**1 tablespoon FILIPPO BERIO® Extra Virgin Olive Oil**
**½ teaspoon dried oregano leaves**
   **Salt**

In medium saucepan, cook beans in boiling salted water 10 to 15 minutes or until tender. Drain well; cool slightly. In small bowl, whisk together lemon juice, olive oil and oregano. Pour over green beans; toss until lightly coated. Cover; refrigerate several hours or overnight before serving. Season to taste with salt.                  *Makes 6 servings*

NOTE: Salad may also be served as an appetizer.

## HERB SAUCED VEGETABLES

**3 cups fresh vegetables, such as broccoli flowerets,**
   **cauliflowerets, sliced yellow squash, green beans,**
   **carrots and snow peas**
**1 cup chicken broth**
**½ cup prepared HIDDEN VALLEY® The Original Ranch®**
   **Dressing**
**¼ cup chopped fresh parsley**

In large saucepan, steam vegetables separately over boiling chicken broth until crisp-tender, about 5 minutes for each batch. Transfer to heated serving dish. Warm salad dressing and spoon over vegetables. Sprinkle with parsley.
                                   *Makes 4 servings*

*Quick Tip*

When you're in a hurry, select cut-up vegetables from the supermarket salad bar. Most produce sections offer time-saving packaged cauliflower and broccoli florets, matchstick carrots and sliced mushrooms.

## PESTO DOUBLE-STUFFED POTATOES

**4 large Idaho Potatoes, baked**
**½ cup part-skim ricotta cheese**
**⅓ cup prepared pesto**
**¼ teaspoon salt**
**¼ teaspoon pepper**
**Nonstick cooking spray**

1. Preheat oven to 450°F.

2. Cut ½ inch from long side of each potato into bowl; scoop out inside of potato, leaving ¼-inch-thick shell. With fork or potato masher, mash cooked potato in bowl. Stir in ricotta, pesto, salt and pepper until well-blended. Spoon potato mixture into potato shells, dividing evenly, heaping on top if necessary.

3. Lightly spray cookie sheet with nonstick cooking spray; place stuffed potatoes on cookie sheet. Bake until golden brown and heated through, about 10 to 15 minutes.

*Makes 4 servings*

**Preparation/Cooking Time:** 45 minutes

*Favorite recipe from* **Idaho Potato Commission**

## NUTTY VEGETABLE DUO

**1 (10-ounce) package frozen green beans**
**½ (16-ounce) package frozen small whole onions**
**¼ cup toasted slivered almonds**
**2 tablespoons butter or margarine**

1. Combine beans and onions in medium saucepan; cook according to package directions. Drain.

2. Return vegetables to saucepan. Add almonds and butter; stir over low heat until butter is melted and mixture is thoroughly heated. Season with salt and pepper to taste.

*Makes 4 servings*

## Quick Tip

To toast almonds, spread them evenly in a shallow baking pan. Bake them at 350°F for 8 to 10 minutes or until they are lightly toasted. Be sure to stir them occasionally.

## *Express Recipe*

For a quick way to dress up carrots, toss steamed or boiled baby carrots with melted butter, black pepper and a little ground nutmeg.

# ROSEMARY GARLIC POTATOES

**4 large red skin potatoes, cut into wedges (about 2 pounds)**
**1½ teaspoons dried rosemary leaves**
**1 teaspoon garlic powder**
**2 tablespoons FLEISCHMANN'S® Original Margarine, melted**

1. Toss potatoes with rosemary and garlic in large bowl; arrange on lightly greased baking dish in single layer. Drizzle with melted margarine.

2. Broil 4 inches from heat source for 25 to 30 minutes or until tender, turning potatoes over once.

*Makes 4 servings*

**Preparation Time:** 15 minutes
**Cook Time:** 25 minutes
**Total Time:** 40 minutes

# LEMON PARMESAN CAULIFLOWER

**1 medium head cauliflower**
**Juice of 1 fresh SUNKIST® lemon**
**2 to 3 tablespoons butter or margarine, melted**
**2 to 3 tablespoons grated Parmesan cheese**
**¼ teaspoon paprika**
**Salt and pepper**

In large saucepan, cook cauliflower in 1 inch boiling water with juice of ½ lemon 5 to 10 minutes for flowerets, 15 to 20 minutes for whole cauliflower or until tender; drain. To serve, sprinkle cauliflower with remaining juice of ½ lemon and butter. Combine Parmesan cheese and paprika; sprinkle over cauliflower. Sprinkle with salt and pepper to taste. Garnish with lemon cartwheel twists and parsley, if desired.

*Makes 4 to 6 servings*

# CHUTNEY'D SQUASH CIRCLES

**2 acorn squash (1 pound each)**
**2 tablespoons butter or margarine**
**½ cup prepared chutney**
**Purple kale and scented geranium leaves for garnish***

*\*Use only non-toxic leaves.*

1. Preheat oven to 400°F. Slice tip and stem end from squash. Scoop out and discard seeds. Cut squash crosswise into ¾-inch rings.

2. Tear off 18-inch square of heavy-duty foil. Center foil in 13×9-inch baking dish. Dot foil with butter and place squash on butter, slightly overlapping rings. Spoon chutney over slices and sprinkle with 2 tablespoons water.

3. Bring foil on long sides of pan together in center, folding over to make tight seam. Fold ends to form tight seal.

4. Bake 20 to 30 minutes until squash is fork-tender. Transfer to warm serving plate. Pour pan drippings over squash. Garnish, if desired.              *Makes 4 side-dish servings*

# POTATOES AU GRATIN

**1½ pounds red bliss potatoes (about 4 to 5), parboiled**
**1 (6-ounce) package FLEUR DE LAIT® Premium Light Spreading Cheese, any savory flavor**
**3 tablespoons chicken broth**
**3 tablespoons grated Parmesan cheese**

Preheat oven to 350°F.

Slice potatoes into ¼-inch slices. Lay half the potatoes in 8×8×2-inch casserole that has been sprayed with nonstick cooking spray.

Combine Fleur de Lait with chicken broth; mix until smooth.

Pour half the cheese mixture over potatoes. Top with remaining potatoes and cheese mixture.

Sprinkle with Parmesan cheese.

Bake potatoes 25 to 30 minutes or until top is golden.
*Makes 12 side-dish servings*

## Express Recipe

For Garlicky Green Beans, simply sauté 1 minced clove of garlic in 1 tablespoon of olive oil until garlic is tender but not brown. Toss this flavored oil with about 1 pound of steamed or boiled cut green beans. Season to taste with salt and black pepper.

# HONEY-MUSTARD ROASTED POTATOES

**4 large baking potatoes (about 2 pounds)**
**½ cup Dijon mustard**
**¼ cup honey**
**½ teaspoon crushed dried thyme leaves**
**Salt and pepper to taste**

Peel potatoes and cut each into 6 to 8 pieces. Cover potatoes with salted water in large saucepan. Bring to a boil over medium-high heat. Cook potatoes 12 to 15 minutes or until just tender. Drain. Combine mustard, honey and thyme in small bowl. Toss potatoes with honey-thyme mustard in large bowl until evenly coated. Arrange potatoes on foil-lined baking sheet coated with nonstick cooking spray. Bake at 375°F 20 minutes or until potatoes begin to brown around edges. Season to taste with salt and pepper.

*Makes 4 servings*

*Favorite recipe from* **National Honey Board**

# ROASTED GARLIC MASHED POTATOES

**3 pounds all-purpose potatoes, peeled, if desired, and cut into chunks**
**1 jar (1 pound) RAGÚ® Cheese Creations!® Roasted Garlic Parmesan Sauce**
**¼ cup chopped fresh parsley (optional)**
**½ teaspoon salt**
**¼ teaspoon ground black pepper**

In 3-quart saucepan, cover potatoes with water. Bring to a boil over high heat. Reduce heat to low and simmer uncovered 20 minutes or until potatoes are very tender; drain. Return potatoes to saucepan; mash potatoes with Ragú Cheese Creations! Sauce, parsley, salt and pepper.

*Makes 12 servings*

## CUCUMBER SALAD

**2 cucumbers**
**½ cup plain nonfat yogurt**
**1 teaspoon dried mint**
**½ teaspoon sugar**

Slice cucumbers. Combine yogurt, mint and sugar in small bowl. Toss cucumbers in yogurt mixture. Serve immediately.

*Makes 4 servings*

*Favorite recipe from* **The Sugar Association, Inc.**

## QUICK POTATO SALAD

**2 pounds small red potatoes, cooked**
**½ cup sliced green onions**
**1 cup HIDDEN VALLEY® The Original Ranch® Dressing with Bacon**
**Paprika or black pepper**
**Chives**

When cool enough to handle, cut potatoes into 1-inch cubes. In large bowl, combine potatoes, onions and salad dressing; toss gently. Dust top with paprika. Garnish with chives. Serve warm or at room temperature.

*Makes 4 to 6 servings*

## DILLED CARROT SALAD

**¼ teaspoon dill weed**
**1 can (8¼ ounces) DEL MONTE® Sliced Carrots, drained**
**5 cups torn romaine lettuce**
**Honey Dijon dressing**

1. Sprinkle dill over carrots in large bowl.

2. Add lettuce; toss with dressing.

*Makes 4 servings*

**Prep Time:** 5 minutes

# FRENCHED BEANS WITH CELERY

**¾ pound fresh green beans, trimmed**
**2 ribs celery, cut diagonally into thin slices**
**2 tablespoons butter, melted**
**2 tablespoons toasted sunflower seeds***
  **Celery leaves and carrot slices for garnish**

*\*To toast sunflower seeds, heat ½ teaspoon oil in small skillet over medium heat. Add shelled sunflower seeds; cook and stir 3 minutes or until lightly browned, shaking pan constantly. Remove to paper towels.*

1. Slice beans lengthwise; set aside.

2. Bring 1 inch of water in 2-quart saucepan to a boil over high heat. Add beans and celery. Cover; reduce heat to medium-low. Simmer 8 minutes or until beans are crisp-tender; drain.

3. Toss beans and celery with butter. Transfer to warm serving dish. Sprinkle with sunflower seeds. Garnish, if desired. Serve immediately.          *Makes 6 side-dish servings*

# SESAME BROCCOLI

**1 bag (16 ounces) BIRDS EYE® frozen Broccoli Cuts**
**1 tablespoon sesame seeds**
**1 tablespoon oil**
  **Dash soy sauce (optional)**

• Cook broccoli according to package directions.

• Cook sesame seeds in oil 1 to 2 minutes or until golden brown, stirring frequently.

• Toss broccoli with sesame seed mixture. Add soy sauce, salt and pepper to taste.          *Makes 4 to 6 servings*

**Prep Time:** 1 minute
**Cook Time:** 8 to 9 minutes

## Quick Tip

Celery ribs can have tough strings. You can easily remove them by grasping the ends of the strings at the top of the cut ribs between your thumb and a paring knife. Then, pull the strings down the length of the ribs to remove them.

## COB CORN IN BARBECUE BUTTER

**4 ears fresh corn, shucked**
**2 tablespoons butter or margarine, softened**
**½ teaspoon dry barbecue seasoning**
**¼ teaspoon salt**
**Cherry tomato wedges and Italian parsley for garnish**

1. Pour 1 inch of water into large saucepan or skillet. (Do not add salt, as it will make corn tough.) Bring to a boil over medium-high heat. Add ears; cover. Cook 4 to 6 minutes until kernels are slightly crisp when pierced with fork.*

2. Remove corn with tongs to warm serving platter. Blend butter, barbecue seasoning and salt in small bowl until smooth. Serve immediately with corn. Garnish, if desired.

*Makes 4 side-dish servings*

*\*Length of cooking time depends on size and age of corn.*

## SOUPER STUFFING

**2 packages KNORR® Recipe Classics™ Vegetable or French Onion Soup, Dip and Recipe Mix**
**4 cups water**
**½ cup (1 stick) margarine or butter**
**1 package (14 to 15 ounces) bread stuffing mix, any flavor**

• Preheat oven to 350°F. Lightly grease 3-quart casserole. In large saucepan, combine recipe mix, water and margarine; stirring occasionally, heat to boiling. Remove from heat.

• Stir in stuffing mix just until evenly moistened. Spoon into prepared casserole.

• Bake 30 minutes or until lightly browned and heated through.                      *Makes 12 servings*

SAUSAGE STUFFING: In step 1, sauté ½ pound crumbled sausage in saucepan before adding water and recipe mix. Reduce margarine to 4 tablespoons.

**Prep Time:** 10 minutes
**Cook Time:** 30 minutes

# SCALLOPED GARLIC POTATOES

**3 medium all-purpose potatoes, peeled and thinly sliced
(about 1½ pounds)
1 envelope LIPTON® RECIPE SECRETS® Savory Herb with
Garlic Soup Mix\*
1 cup (½ pint) whipping or heavy cream
½ cup water**

*\*Also terrific with LIPTON® RECIPE SECRETS® Savory Herb.*

1. Preheat oven to 375°F. In lightly greased 2-quart shallow baking dish, arrange potatoes. In medium bowl, blend remaining ingredients; pour over potatoes.

2. Bake, uncovered, 45 minutes or until potatoes are tender.

*Makes 4 servings*

# OVEN-ROASTED ASPARAGUS

**1 bunch (12 to 14 ounces) asparagus spears
1 tablespoon olive oil
¼ cup shredded Asiago or Parmesan cheese**

1. Preheat oven to 425°F.

2. Trim off and discard tough ends of asparagus spears. Peel stem ends of asparagus with vegetable peeler, if desired. Arrange asparagus in shallow baking dish. Drizzle oil onto asparagus; turn stalks to coat. Sprinkle with salt and pepper, to taste.

3. Bake until asparagus is tender, about 12 to 18 minutes depending on thickness of asparagus. Chop or leave spears whole. Sprinkle with cheese.

*Makes 4 servings*

## EASY PINEAPPLE SLAW

**1 can (15¼ ounces) DEL MONTE® Pineapple Tidbits
   In Its Own Juice
⅓ cup mayonnaise
2 tablespoons vinegar
6 cups coleslaw mix or shredded cabbage**

1. Drain pineapple, reserving 3 tablespoons juice.

2. Combine reserved juice, mayonnaise and vinegar; toss with pineapple and coleslaw mix. Season with salt and pepper to taste, if desired.     *Makes 4 to 6 servings*

**Prep Time:** 5 minutes

## GRILLED BANANA SQUASH WITH RUM & BROWN SUGAR

**2 pounds banana squash or butternut squash
2 tablespoons dark rum or apple juice
2 tablespoons melted butter
2 tablespoons brown sugar**

Cut squash into 4 pieces; discard seeds. Place squash in microwavable baking dish. Cover with vented plastic wrap. Microwave at HIGH 5 to 7 minutes, turning once. Discard plastic wrap; pierce flesh of squash with fork at 1-inch intervals. Place squash in foil pan. Combine rum and butter; brush over squash. Sprinkle with sugar. Grill squash on covered grill over medium KINGSFORD® Briquets 20 to 30 minutes until squash is tender.     *Makes 4 servings*

*Express Recipe*

Bake medium, pierced sweet potatoes at 400°F for 45 minutes or until they are tender. Or, cook them in a microwave oven following the manufacturer's directions. Cool the potatoes slightly, cut them open and serve them with sour cream or plain yogurt and a sprinkling of brown sugar, salt and black pepper.

# ORIGINAL GREEN BEAN CASSEROLE

**1 can (10¾ ounces) condensed cream of mushroom soup**
**¾ cup milk**
**⅛ teaspoon ground black pepper**
**2 packages (9 ounces each) frozen cut green beans,**
    **thawed and drained *or* 2 cans (14½ ounces each)**
    **cut green beans, drained**
**1⅓ cups *French's*® French Fried Onions, divided**

Preheat oven to 350°F. Combine soup, milk and ground pepper in 1½-quart casserole; stir until well blended. Stir in beans and ⅔ *cup* French Fried Onions.

Bake, uncovered, 30 minutes or until hot. Stir; sprinkle with remaining ⅔ *cup* onions. Bake 5 minutes or until onions are golden.                                    *Makes 6 servings*

MICROWAVE DIRECTIONS: Prepare green bean mixture as above; pour into 1½-quart microwave-safe casserole. Cook, covered, on HIGH 8 to 10 minutes or until heated through. Stir beans halfway through cooking time. Top with remaining French Fried Onions; cook, uncovered, 1 minute. Let stand 5 minutes.

**Prep Time:** 5 minutes
**Cook Time:** 35 minutes

# ORIGINAL RANCH® GRILLED BREAD

**1 packet (1 ounce) HIDDEN VALLEY® The Original Ranch®**
    **Salad Dressing & Seasoning Mix**
**½ cup butter**
**2 loaves French bread, cut in half lengthwise**

Soften butter and stir in dressing mix. Spread on bread. Grill or broil until golden.                          *Makes 2 loaves*

MOZZARELLA BREAD VARIATION: Sprinkle ½ cup shredded mozzarella cheese on top before grilling or broiling.

## Express Recipe

Prepare a combination of sliced zucchini and yellow summer squash by sautéing them in olive oil or butter with chopped onion and diced red bell pepper until all the vegetables are tender. Sprinkle with salt, black pepper and a little grated Parmesan cheese.

## 1–2–3 CHEDDAR BROCCOLI CASSEROLE

**1 jar (1 pound) RAGÚ® Cheese Creations!® Double
  Cheddar Sauce
2 boxes (10 ounces each) frozen broccoli florets, thawed
¼ cup plain or Italian seasoned dry bread crumbs
1 tablespoon margarine or butter, melted**

Preheat oven to 350°F. In 1½-quart casserole, combine Ragú
Cheese Creations! Sauce and broccoli.

Evenly top with bread crumbs combined with margarine.

Bake uncovered 20 minutes or until bread crumbs are golden
and broccoli is tender.                    *Makes 6 servings*

TIP: Substitute your favorite frozen vegetables or vegetable
blend for broccoli florets.

**Prep Time:** 5 minutes
**Cook Time:** 20 minutes

## PINEAPPLE YAM CASSEROLE

**4 medium yams, cooked, peeled and mashed, *or*
    2 (16- or 17-ounce) cans yams, drained and mashed
⅓ cup SMUCKER'S® Pineapple Topping
4 tablespoons butter or margarine, melted, divided
1 tablespoon lemon juice**

Combine yams, pineapple topping, 3 tablespoons butter and
lemon juice; mix well. Brush 1-quart casserole with
remaining 1 tablespoon butter. Spoon yam mixture into
casserole.

Bake at 350°F for 25 minutes or until heated through.

*Makes 4 servings*

---

*Express Recipe*

Steam sliced green cabbage for about 5 minutes or until it is tender. Serve it with a mixture of melted butter, celery salt and black pepper. Adding steamed sliced red cabbage will make your presentation more colorful.

# BROTH—BRAISED BRUSSELS SPROUTS

**1 pound fresh Brussels sprouts**
**½ cup condensed beef broth *or* ½ cup water plus**
**2 teaspoons instant beef bouillon granules**
**1 tablespoon butter or margarine, softened**
**¼ cup freshly grated Parmesan cheese**

1. Trim stems from Brussels sprouts and pull off outer discolored leaves.

2. Use large enough saucepan to allow sprouts to fit in single layer. Place sprouts in saucepan; add broth. Bring to a boil; reduce heat. Cover; simmer about 5 minutes or just until sprouts turn bright green and are crisp-tender.

3. Uncover; simmer until liquid is almost evaporated. Toss cooked sprouts with butter and cheese. Sprinkle with paprika, if desired.                    *Makes 4 side-dish servings*

TIP: For faster, more even cooking, cut an "X" deep into the stem end of each Brussels sprout.

# ALOUETTE® ARTICHOKES

**1 (6.5-ounce) package ALOUETTE® Garlic & Herbs**
**2 (13-ounce) cans artichoke hearts**
**¼ cup bread crumbs**
**Fresh chervil or parsley**

Preheat oven to 350°F.

With thumb, make an impression in each artichoke heart. Fill each artichoke with 1 teaspoon Alouette and sprinkle with bread crumbs.

Place in baking pan; bake 15 minutes.

Place under broiler until bread crumbs are slightly browned. Garnish with fresh chervil.                    *Makes 6 servings*

# HONEY–GLAZED CARROTS AND PARSNIPS

**½ pound carrots, thinly sliced**
**½ pound parsnips, peeled and thinly sliced**
**¼ cup chopped fresh parsley**
**2 tablespoons honey**
**Additional fresh parsley (optional)**

Steam carrots and parsnips over simmering water in large saucepan 3 to 4 minutes or until crisp-tender. Rinse under cold running water; drain. Combine carrots, parsnips, parsley and honey in same saucepan. Cook over medium heat just until heated through. Garnish with additional parsley, if desired. Serve immediately. *Makes 6 (⅔-cup) servings*

# LEMONY STEAMED BROCCOLI

**1 pound broccoli**
**1 tablespoon butter**
**2 teaspoons lemon juice**

1. Break broccoli into florets. Discard large stems. Trim smaller stems; cut stems into thin slices.

2. Place 2 to 3 inches of water and steamer basket in large saucepan; bring water to a boil.

3. Add broccoli; cover. Steam 6 minutes or until crisp-tender.

4. Place broccoli in serving bowl. Add butter and lemon juice; toss lightly to coat. Season with salt and pepper to taste. *Makes 4 servings*

## SWEET & TANGY COLESLAW

**1 small bag (16 ounces) shredded cabbage**
**½ cup mayonnaise**
**½ cup *French's*® Sweet & Tangy Honey Mustard**

1. Combine ingredients. Chill until ready to serve.
*Makes 6 to 8 servings*

**Prep Time:** 5 minutes

## LINGUINE WITH OIL AND GARLIC

**½ cup FILIPPO BERIO® Extra Virgin Olive Oil, divided**
**10 cloves garlic, minced**
**¾ pound uncooked linguine**
**¼ teaspoon black pepper**
**¼ teaspoon salt (optional)**

1. Heat 2 tablespoons olive oil in small saucepan over medium heat. Add garlic; cook and stir until lightly browned. Remove from heat; set aside.

2. Cook linguine according to package directions until tender. *Do not overcook.*

3. Drain pasta; return to saucepan. Toss with garlic and olive oil mixture, remaining 6 tablespoons olive oil, pepper and salt, if desired.
*Makes 4 servings*

*Quick Tip*

Purchasing ready-to-eat salad greens, shredded cabbage and coleslaw mix is a great way to save preparation steps in the kitchen. It can also provide a wider variety of greens.

# Cookies in a Flash

## NUTTY LEMON CRESCENTS

**1 package (18 ounces) refrigerated sugar cookie dough**
**1 cup chopped pecans, toasted***
**1 tablespoon grated lemon peel**
**1½ cups powdered sugar, divided**

*\*To toast pecans, spread in a single layer on a baking sheet. Bake in a preheated 350°F oven 8 to 10 minutes or until pecans are golden brown, stirring frequently.*

1. Preheat oven to 375°F. Remove dough from wrapper according to package directions.

2. Combine dough, pecans and lemon peel in large bowl. Stir until thoroughly blended. Shape level tablespoonfuls of dough into crescent shapes. Place 2 inches apart on ungreased cookie sheets. Bake 8 to 9 minutes or until set and very lightly browned. Cool 2 minutes on cookie sheets. Remove to wire racks.

3. Place 1 cup powdered sugar in shallow bowl. Roll warm cookies in powdered sugar. Cool completely. Sift remaining ½ cup powdered sugar over cookies just before serving.

*Makes about 4 dozen cookies*

## SCRUMPTIOUS MINTED BROWNIES

**1 (21-ounce) package DUNCAN HINES® Family-Style Chewy Fudge Brownie Mix**
**1 egg**
**⅓ cup water**
**⅓ cup vegetable oil**
**48 chocolate crème de menthe candy wafers, divided**

1. Preheat oven to 350°F. Grease bottom only of 13×9-inch pan.

2. Combine brownie mix, egg, water and oil in large bowl. Stir with spoon until well blended, about 50 strokes. Spread in prepared pan. Bake at 350°F for 25 minutes or until set. Place 30 candy wafers evenly over hot brownies. Let stand for 1 minute to melt. Spread candy wafers to frost brownies. Score frosting into 36 bars by running tip of knife through melted candy. (Do not cut through brownies.) Cut remaining 18 candy wafers in half lengthwise; place halves on each scored bar. Cool completely. Cut into bars.

*Makes 36 brownies*

## BROWN SUGAR SHORTBREAD

**1 cup (2 sticks) I CAN'T BELIEVE IT'S NOT BUTTER!® Spread**
**¾ cup firmly packed light brown sugar**
**2 cups all-purpose flour**
**⅓ cup semisweet chocolate chips, melted**

Preheat oven to 325°F. Grease 9-inch round cake pan; set aside.

In large bowl, with electric mixer, beat I Can't Believe It's Not Butter!® Spread and brown sugar until light and fluffy, about 5 minutes. Gradually add flour and beat on low until blended. Spread mixture into prepared pan and press into even layer. With knife, score surface into 8 pie-shaped wedges.

Bake 30 minutes or until lightly golden. On wire rack, cool 20 minutes; remove from pan and cool completely. To serve, pour melted chocolate into small plastic storage bag. Snip corner and drizzle chocolate over shortbread. Cut into wedges.

*Makes 8 servings*

# SANDWICH COOKIES

**1 package (20 ounces) refrigerated cookie dough,
      any flavor
All-purpose flour (optional)
Any combination of colored frostings, peanut butter
      or assorted ice creams for filling
Colored sprinkles, chocolate-covered raisins, miniature
      candy-coated chocolate pieces and other assorted
      small candies for decoration**

1. Preheat oven to 350°F. Grease cookie sheets.

2. Remove dough from wrapper according to package directions. Cut dough into 4 equal sections. Reserve 1 section; refrigerate remaining 3 sections.

3. Roll reserved dough to ¼-inch thickness. Sprinkle with flour to minimize sticking, if necessary.

4. Cut out cookies using ¾-inch round or fluted cookie cutter. Transfer cookies to prepared cookie sheets, placing about 2 inches apart. Repeat steps with remaining dough.

5. Bake 8 to 11 minutes or until edges are lightly browned. Remove to wire racks; cool completely.

6. To make sandwich, spread about 1 tablespoon desired filling on flat side of 1 cookie to within ¼ inch of edge. Top with second cookie, pressing gently. Roll side of sandwich in desired decorations. Repeat with remaining cookies.

*Makes about 20 to 24 sandwich cookies*

# POLKA DOT MACAROONS

**1 (14-ounce) bag (5 cups) shredded coconut
1 (14-ounce) can sweetened condensed milk
½ cup all-purpose flour
1¾ cups "M&M's"® Chocolate Mini Baking Bits**

Preheat oven to 350°F. Grease cookie sheets; set aside. In large bowl combine coconut, condensed milk and flour until well blended. Stir in "M&M's"® Chocolate Mini Baking Bits. Drop by rounded tablespoonfuls about 2 inches apart onto prepared cookie sheets. Bake 8 to 10 minutes or until edges are golden. Cool completely on wire racks. Store in tightly covered container. *Makes about 5 dozen cookies*

# CHOCOLATE–CARAMEL S'MORES

**12 chocolate wafer cookies or chocolate graham
   cracker squares
2 tablespoons fat-free caramel topping
6 large marshmallows**

1. Prepare coals for grilling. Place 6 wafer cookies top down on plate. Spread 1 teaspoon caramel topping in center of each wafer to within about ¼ inch of edge.

2. Spear 1 to 2 marshmallows onto long wood-handled skewer.* Hold several inches above coals 3 to 5 minutes or until marshmallows are golden and very soft, turning slowly. Push 1 marshmallow off into center of caramel. Top with plain wafer. Repeat with remaining marshmallows and wafers.                                         *Makes 6 servings*

*If wood-handled skewers are unavailable, use oven mitt to protect hand from heat.*

# QUICK NO–BAKE BROWNIES

**1 cup finely chopped nuts, divided
2 (1-ounce) squares unsweetened chocolate
1 (14-ounce) can EAGLE BRAND® Sweetened Condensed
   Milk (NOT evaporated milk)
2 to 2½ cups vanilla wafer crumbs (about 48 to
   60 wafers)**

1. Grease 9-inch square pan with butter. Sprinkle ¼ cup nuts evenly over bottom of pan. In heavy saucepan over low heat, melt chocolate with Eagle Brand. Cook and stir until mixture thickens, about 10 minutes.

2. Remove from heat; stir in crumbs and ½ cup nuts. Spread evenly in prepared pan.

3. Top with remaining ¼ cup nuts. Chill 4 hours or until firm. Cut into squares. Store loosely covered at room temperature.                                         *Makes 24 brownies*

**Prep Time:** 15 minutes
**Chill Time:** 4 hours

## Quick Tip

For easy removal of brownies, line the baking pan with foil and leave at least 3 inches hanging over each end. Use the foil to lift out the treats. Place them on a cutting board and carefully remove the foil. Then, simply cut the brownies into pieces. The best part is there's no pan to wash!

# THUMBPRINTS

**1 package (20 ounces) refrigerated sugar or chocolate cookie dough**
**All-purpose flour (optional)**
**¾ cup plus 1 tablespoon fruit preserves, any flavor**

1. Grease cookie sheets. Remove dough from wrapper according to package directions. Sprinkle with flour to minimize sticking, if necessary.

2. Cut dough into 26 (1-inch) slices. Roll slices into balls, sprinkling with additional flour, if necessary. Place balls 2 inches apart on prepared cookie sheets. Press deep indentation in center of each ball with thumb. Freeze dough 20 minutes.

3. Preheat oven to 350°F. Bake cookies 12 to 13 minutes or until edges are light golden brown (cookies will have started to puff up and lose their shape). Quickly press down indentation using tip of teaspoon.

4. Return to oven 2 to 3 minutes or until cookies are golden brown and set. Cool cookies completely on cookie sheets. Fill each indentation with about 1½ teaspoons preserves.

*Makes 26 cookies*

# MARASCHINO BROWNIES

**1 (21½- to 23½-ounce) package brownie mix (13×9 pan size)**
**1 (8-ounce) container plain low-fat yogurt**
**1 (10-ounce) jar maraschino cherries, drained**

Prepare brownie mix according to package directions, adding yogurt with liquid ingredients; mix well. Stir in cherries. Spoon batter into greased and floured 13×9×2-inch baking pan. Make sure cherries are evenly distributed.

Bake in a preheated 350°F oven 28 to 30 minutes. *Do not overbake.* Brownies will be moist and cannot be tested with wooden pick.

*Makes 2 dozen bars*

*Favorite recipe from* **Cherry Marketing Institute**

# DOMINO COOKIES

**1 package (20 ounces) refrigerated sugar cookie dough**
**All-purpose flour (optional)**
**½ cup semisweet chocolate chips**

1. Preheat oven to 350°F. Grease cookie sheets.

2. Remove dough from wrapper according to package directions. Cut dough into 4 equal sections. Reserve 1 section; refrigerate remaining 3 sections.

3. Roll reserved dough to ⅛-inch thickness. Sprinkle with flour to minimize sticking, if necessary. Cut out 9 (2½×1¾-inch) rectangles using sharp knife. Place 2 inches apart on prepared cookie sheets.

4. Score each cookie across middle with sharp knife. Gently press chocolate chips, point side down, into dough to resemble various dominos. Repeat with remaining dough, scraps and chocolate chips.

5. Bake 8 to 10 minutes or until edges are light golden brown. Remove to wire racks; cool completely.

*Makes 3 dozen cookies*

# CHOCOLATE WALNUT MERINGUES

**3 egg whites**
**Pinch of salt**
**¾ cup sugar**
**½ cup good-quality Dutch-processed cocoa**
**⅓ cup finely chopped California walnuts**

Preheat oven to 350°F. Place egg whites and salt in large mixing bowl. Beat with electric mixer or wire whisk until soft peaks form. Gradually add sugar, beating until stiff peaks form. Sift cocoa over peaks and fold into egg white mixture with walnuts. Spoon mounds about 1 inch in diameter and about 1 inch apart onto parchment-lined cookie sheets. Bake 20 minutes or until dry to the touch. Let cool completely before removing from cookie sheets. Store in airtight container.

*Makes 48 cookies*

*Favorite recipe from* **Walnut Marketing Board**

# CHOCOLATE MINT RAVIOLI COOKIES

**1 package (15 ounces) refrigerated pie crusts**
**1 bar (7 ounces) cookies 'n' mint chocolate candy**
**1 egg**
**1 tablespoon water**
**Powdered sugar**

1. Preheat oven to 400°F. Unfold 1 pie crust on lightly floured surface. Roll into 13-inch circle. Using 2½-inch cutters, cut pastry into 24 circles, rerolling scraps if necessary. Repeat with remaining pie crust.

2. Separate candy bar into pieces marked on bar. Cut each chocolate piece in half. Beat egg and water together in small bowl with fork. Brush half of pastry circles lightly with egg mixture. Place 1 piece of chocolate in center of each circle (there will be some candy bar left over). Top with remaining pastry circles. Seal edges with tines of fork.

3. Place on *ungreased* baking sheets. Brush with egg mixture.

4. Bake 8 to 10 minutes or until golden brown. Remove from cookie sheets; cool completely on wire racks. Dust with powdered sugar. *Makes 2 dozen cookies*

**Prep and Cook Time:** 30 minutes

# SKIPPY QUICK COOKIES

**1 cup SKIPPY® Creamy or Super Chunk Peanut Butter**
**1 cup sugar**
**1 egg, slightly beaten**
**1 teaspoon vanilla extract**

Preheat oven to 325°F. In medium bowl, combine all ingredients. Shape dough into 1-inch balls. On *ungreased* cookie sheets, arrange cookies 2 inches apart. With fork, gently flatten each cookie and press crisscross pattern into top.

Bake 8 minutes or until lightly browned and slightly puffed. Immediately top, if desired, with sprinkles, chocolate chips or chocolate candies. On wire rack, cool completely before removing from cookie sheets. *Makes 2 dozen cookies*

**Prep Time:** 10 minutes
**Cook Time:** 8 minutes

# DOUBLE CHOCOLATE SANDWICH COOKIES

**1 package (18 ounces) refrigerated sugar cookie dough**
**1 bar (3½ to 4 ounces) bittersweet chocolate candy, chopped**
**2 teaspoons butter**
**¾ cup milk chocolate chips**

1. Preheat oven to 350°F.

2. Cut well-chilled cookie dough into ¼-inch-thick slices. Arrange slices 2 inches apart on ungreased cookie sheets. Cut ½- to 1-inch circles out of center of half of cookies.

3. Bake cookies 10 to 12 minutes or until edges are golden brown. Let stand on cookie sheets 2 minutes; transfer to wire racks. Cool completely.

4. Place bittersweet chocolate and butter in heavy small saucepan. Heat over low heat, stirring frequently, until chocolate is melted. Spread chocolate over bottoms of cookies without holes. Immediately top each chocolate-coated cookie with cookie with hole.

5. Place milk chocolate chips in small heavy plastic freezer bag; seal bag. Microwave at MEDIUM (50%) 1½ minutes. Turn bag over; microwave 1 to 1½ minutes or until melted. Knead bag until chocolate is smooth.

6. Cut very tiny corner off bag; drizzle chocolate decoratively over sandwich cookies. Let stand until chocolate is set, about 30 minutes.                    *Makes 16 sandwich cookies*

**Quick Tip**

To cut 1-inch circles from the center of these cookies, use the wide end of a pastry bag tip, the removable center of a doughnut cutter or a melon baller.

# CHOCOLATE CHIP MACAROONS

**2½ cups flaked coconut**
**⅔ cup mini semisweet chocolate chips**
**⅔ cup sweetened condensed milk**
**1 teaspoon vanilla**

Preheat oven to 350°F. Grease cookie sheets. Combine coconut, chocolate chips, milk and vanilla in medium bowl; mix until well blended. Drop dough by rounded teaspoonfuls 2 inches apart onto prepared cookie sheets. Press dough gently with back of spoon to flatten slightly. Bake 10 to 12 minutes or until light golden brown. Let cookies stand on cookie sheets 1 minute. Remove cookies to wire racks; cool completely. *Makes about 3½ dozen cookies*

# BUTTER FUDGE FINGERS

**1 (21-ounce) package DUNCAN HINES® Family-Style Chewy Fudge Brownie Mix**
**1 container DUNCAN HINES® Creamy Home-Style Buttercream Frosting**
**¼ cup semisweet chocolate chips**
**1½ teaspoons shortening plus additional for greasing**

1. Preheat oven to 350°F. Grease bottom only of 13×9×2-inch pan.

2. Prepare, bake and cool brownies following package directions for basic recipe chewy brownies. Spread with Buttercream frosting.

3. Place chocolate chips and shortening in small resealable plastic bag; seal. Microwave at HIGH (100% power) 30 seconds, adding 15 to 30 seconds more if needed. Knead until blended. Snip pinpoint hole in corner of bag. Drizzle chocolate over frosting. Allow chocolate to set before cutting into bars. *Makes 18 brownies*

TIP: Another method for melting the chocolate and shortening in the sealed bag is to place it in a bowl of hot water for several minutes. Dry the bag with a paper towel. Knead, snip and pipe as directed above.

## Express Recipe

For a spur-of-the moment cookie that will impress everyone, dip purchased shortbread cookies in melted chocolate. Heat 1 cup of semisweet chocolate chips and 2 teaspoons shortening in a small bowl in a microwave oven at HIGH for 1 minute, then stir. Microwave in 15 second increments until the chips are melted when stirred. Dip half of each cookie into the chocolate mixture and place them on a wire rack over waxed paper until the chocolate is set. The chocolate mixture is enough to half-coat about 18 to 20 cookies.

# SMUSHY COOKIES

**1 package (20 ounces) refrigerated cookie dough,
   any flavor
All-purpose flour (optional)**

**Fillings**
**Peanut butter, multi-colored miniature marshmallows,
   assorted colored sprinkles, chocolate-covered raisins
   and caramel candy squares**

1. Preheat oven to 350°F. Grease cookie sheets.

2. Remove dough from wrapper according to package directions. Cut into 4 equal sections. Reserve 1 section; refrigerate remaining 3 sections.

3. Roll out reserved dough to ¼-inch thickness. Sprinkle with flour to minimize sticking, if necessary. Cut out cookies using 2½-inch round cookie cutter. Transfer to prepared cookie sheets. Repeat with remaining dough, working with 1 section at a time.

4. Bake 8 to 11 minutes or until edges are light golden brown. Remove to wire racks; cool completely.

5. To make sandwich, spread about 1½ tablespoons peanut butter on bottom of 1 cookie to within ¼ inch of edge. Sprinkle with miniature marshmallows and candy pieces. Top with second cookie, pressing gently. Repeat with remaining cookies and fillings.

6. Just before serving, place sandwiches on paper towels. Microwave at HIGH 15 to 25 seconds or until fillings become soft.               *Makes about 8 to 10 sandwich cookies*

# CHOCOLATE MACADAMIA CHIPPERS

**1 package (18 ounces) refrigerated chocolate chip
    cookie dough
3 tablespoons unsweetened cocoa powder
½ cup coarsely chopped macadamia nuts
    Powdered sugar (optional)**

1. Preheat oven to 375°F. Remove dough from wrapper according to package directions.

2. Place dough in medium bowl; stir in cocoa until well blended. (Dough may be kneaded lightly, if desired.) Stir in nuts. Drop by heaping tablespoons 2 inches apart onto ungreased cookie sheets.

3. Bake 9 to 11 minutes or until almost set. Transfer to wire racks to cool completely. Dust lightly with powdered sugar, if desired.                     *Makes 2 dozen cookies*

# COCONUT MACAROONS

**1 (14-ounce) can EAGLE BRAND® Sweetened Condensed
    Milk (NOT evaporated milk)
2 teaspoons vanilla extract
1 to 1½ teaspoons almond extract
2 (7-ounce) packages flaked coconut (5⅓ cups)**

1. Preheat oven to 325°F. Line cookie sheets with foil; grease and flour foil. Set aside.

2. In large mixing bowl, combine Eagle Brand, vanilla and almond extract. Stir in coconut. Drop by rounded teaspoonfuls onto prepared sheets; with spoon, slightly flatten each mound.

3. Bake 15 to 17 minutes or until golden. Remove from cookie sheets; cool on wire racks. Store loosely covered at room temperature.            *Makes about 4 dozen cookies*

**Prep Time:** 10 minutes
**Bake Time:** 15 to 17 minutes

# SURPRISE COOKIES

**1 package (18 ounces) refrigerated sugar cookie dough**
**All-purpose flour (optional)**
**Any combination of walnut halves, whole almonds, chocolate-covered raisins or caramel candy squares for filling**
**Assorted colored sugars**

1. Grease cookie sheets. Remove dough from wrapper according to package directions. Divide dough into 4 equal sections. Reserve 1 section; cover and refrigerate remaining 3 sections.

2. Roll reserved dough to ¼-inch thickness. Sprinkle with flour to minimize sticking, if necessary. Cut out 3-inch square cookie with sharp knife. Transfer cookie to prepared cookie sheet.

3. Place desired "surprise" filling in center of cookie. (If using caramel candy square, place so that caramel forms diamond shape within square.)

4. Bring up 4 corners of dough towards center; pinch gently to seal. Repeat steps with remaining dough and fillings, placing cookies about 2 inches apart on prepared cookie sheets. Sprinkle with colored sugar, if desired. Freeze cookies 20 minutes. Meanwhile, preheat oven to 350°F.

5. Bake 9 to 11 minutes or until edges are lightly browned. Remove to wire racks; cool completely.

*Makes about 14 cookies*

# WALNUT MERINGUES

**3 egg whites**
**Pinch salt**
**¾ cup sugar**
**⅓ cup finely chopped walnuts**

Preheat oven to 350°F. Line cookie sheet with parchment paper. Place egg whites and salt in large bowl. Beat until soft peaks form. Gradually add sugar, beating until stiff peaks form. Gently fold in walnuts. Drop mounds about 1 inch in diameter 1 inch apart onto prepared cookie sheet. Bake 20 minutes or until lightly browned and dry to the touch. Let cool completely before removing from cookie sheet. Store in airtight container.

*Makes 48 cookies*

## Quick Tip

Make extra batches of these simple Surprise Cookies and store them in the freezer in heavy-duty freezer bags. Take out a few at a time for your kids' after-school treats.

# FRUITY COOKIE RINGS AND TWISTS

**1 package (20 ounces) refrigerated sugar cookie dough**
**3 cups fruit-flavored cereal, crushed and divided**

1. Remove dough from wrapper according to package directions. Combine dough and ½ cup crushed cereal in large bowl. Divide dough into 32 balls. Refrigerate 1 hour.

2. Preheat oven to 375°F. Shape dough balls into 6- to 8-inch-long ropes. Roll ropes in remaining cereal to coat; shape into rings or fold in half and twist.

3. Place cookies 2 inches apart on ungreased cookie sheets.

4. Bake 10 to 11 minutes or until lightly browned. Remove to wire racks; cool completely.                    *Makes 32 cookies*

# CREAM CHEESE CHOCOLATE CHIP PASTRY COOKIES

**1 package (17.25 ounces) frozen puff pastry sheets, thawed**
**1 package (8 ounces) cream cheese, softened**
**3 tablespoons granulated sugar**
**1¾ cups (11.5-ounce package) NESTLÉ® TOLL HOUSE® Milk Chocolate Morsels, *divided***

UNFOLD 1 puff pastry sheet on lightly floured surface. Roll out to make 14×10-inch rectangle. Combine cream cheese and sugar in small bowl until smooth. Spread *half* of cream cheese mixture over pastry, leaving 1-inch border on one long side. Sprinkle with *half* of morsels. Roll up puff pastry starting at long side covered with cream cheese. Seal end by moistening with water. Repeat steps with *remaining* ingredients. Refrigerate for 1 hour.

PREHEAT oven to 375°F. Lightly grease cookie sheets or line with parchment paper.

CUT rolls crosswise into 1-inch-thick slices. Place cut side down on prepared cookie sheets.

BAKE for 20 to 25 minutes or until golden brown. Cool on cookie sheets for 2 minutes; remove to wire racks to cool completely.                    *Makes about 2 dozen cookies*

## TOFFEE CREME SANDWICH COOKIES

**1 jar (7 ounces) marshmallow creme**
**¼ cup toffee baking pieces**
**48 (2-inch) sugar or fudge-striped shortbread cookies**
**Red and green sprinkles**

1. Combine marshmallow creme and toffee pieces in medium bowl until well blended. (Mixture will be stiff.)

2. Spread 1 teaspoon marshmallow mixture on bottom of 1 cookie; top with another cookie. Roll side of sandwich cookie in sprinkles. Repeat with remaining marshmallow creme mixture, cookies and sprinkles.

*Makes 2 dozen cookies*

**Prep Time:** 20 minutes

## SNICKERDOODLES

**3 tablespoons sugar**
**1 teaspoon ground cinnamon**
**1 package DUNCAN HINES® Moist Deluxe® Classic Yellow Cake Mix**
**2 eggs**
**¼ cup vegetable oil**

1. Preheat oven to 375°F. Grease cookie sheets. Place sheets of foil on countertop for cooling cookies.

2. Combine sugar and cinnamon in small bowl.

3. Combine cake mix, eggs and oil in large bowl. Stir until well blended. Shape dough into 1-inch balls. Roll in cinnamon-sugar mixture. Place balls 2 inches apart on cookie sheets. Flatten balls with bottom of glass.

4. Bake at 375°F for 8 to 9 minutes or until set. Cool 1 minute on cookie sheets. Remove to foil to cool completely.

*Makes about 3 dozen cookies*

# DUTCH CHOCOLATE MERINGUES

¼ **cup finely chopped pecans**
2½ **tablespoons unsweetened cocoa powder (preferably Dutch process)**
3 **egg whites**
¼ **teaspoon salt**
¾ **cup granulated sugar**
   **Powdered sugar (optional)**

1. Preheat oven to 200°F. Line cookie sheets with foil; grease well. Set aside.

2. Place pecans and cocoa in medium bowl; stir to combine.

3. Beat egg whites and salt in clean large bowl with electric mixer at high speed until light and foamy. Gradually beat in granulated sugar until stiff peaks form.

4. Gently fold pecan mixture into egg white mixture with rubber spatula by gently cutting down to bottom of bowl, scraping up side of bowl, then folding over top of mixture. Repeat until pecan mixture is evenly incorporated.

5. Spoon batter into pastry bag fitted with large plain tip. Pipe 1-inch mounds 2 inches apart on prepared cookie sheets. Bake 1 hour. Turn oven off. *Do not open oven door;* let stand in oven until set, 2 hours or overnight.

6. When cookies are firm, carefully peel cookies from foil. Dust with powdered sugar, if desired. Store loosely covered at room temperature up to 2 days.

*Makes about 6 dozen cookies*

# PEANUT BUTTER SHORTBREADS

½ **cup unsalted butter, softened**
½ **cup granulated sugar**
¼ **cup creamy peanut butter**
2 **cups all-purpose flour**

Preheat oven to 300°F. In bowl, combine all ingredients with your fingers until mixture resembles coarse meal. Press the mixture into an ungreased 8-inch round pan. With a fork, prick decorative wedges in the dough. Bake for about 1 hour or until very lightly browned. Cut into wedges while warm.

*Makes 16 wedge-shaped cookies*

*Favorite recipe from **Peanut Advisory Board***

---

## Quick Tip

To make Meringue Mushrooms, pipe the same number of 1-inch-tall "stems" as mounds. Bake as directed in step 5. When cookies are firm, attach "stems" to "caps" with melted chocolate. Dust with sifted unsweetened cocoa powder.

# CHOCOLATE–PECAN ANGELS

**1 cup mini semisweet chocolate chips**
**1 cup chopped pecans, toasted**
**1 cup sifted powdered sugar**
**1 egg white**

Preheat oven to 350°F. Grease cookie sheets. Combine chips, pecans and powdered sugar in medium bowl. Add egg white; mix well. Drop batter by teaspoonfuls 2 inches apart onto prepared cookie sheets.

Bake 11 to 12 minutes or until edges are light golden brown. Let cookies stand on cookie sheets 1 minute. Remove cookies to wire racks; cool completely.

*Makes about 3 dozen cookies*

# HOLIDAY PEPPERMINT SLICES

**1 package (18 ounces) refrigerated sugar cookie dough**
**¼ teaspoon peppermint extract, divided**
**Red food coloring**
**Green food coloring**

1. Remove dough from wrapper according to package directions. Cut dough into thirds.

2. Combine ⅓ of dough, ⅛ teaspoon peppermint extract and enough red food coloring to make dough desired shade of red. Knead dough until evenly tinted.

3. Repeat with second ⅓ of dough, remaining ⅛ teaspoon peppermint extract and green food coloring.

4. To assemble, shape each portion of dough into 8-inch roll. Place red roll beside green roll; press together slightly. Place plain roll on top. Press rolls together to form one tri-colored roll; wrap in plastic wrap. Refrigerate 2 hours or overnight.

5. Preheat oven to 350°F.

6. Cut dough into ¼-inch-thick slices. Place 2 inches apart on ungreased cookie sheets. Bake 8 to 9 minutes or until set but not browned. Cool 1 minute on cookie sheets. Cool completely on wire racks. *Makes 2½ dozen cookies*

## Quick Tip

Add some pizzazz to these Cookie Cups by filling them with a mixture of prepared fruit-flavored gelatin combined with prepared pudding or nondairy whipped topping. For convenience, snack-size gelatins and puddings can be found at the supermarket, so there's no need to make them from scratch.

# COOKIE CUPS

**1 package (20 ounces) refrigerated sugar cookie dough**
**All-purpose flour (optional)**
**Prepared pudding, nondairy whipped topping, maraschino cherries, jelly beans, assorted sprinkles and small candies**

1. Grease 12 (2¾-inch) muffin cups.

2. Remove dough from wrapper according to package directions. Sprinkle dough with flour to minimize sticking, if necessary.

3. Cut dough into 12 equal pieces; roll into balls. Place 1 ball in bottom of each muffin cup. Press dough halfway up sides of muffin cups, making indentation in centers.

4. Freeze muffin cups 15 minutes. Preheat oven to 350°F.

5. Bake 15 to 17 minutes or until golden brown. Cookies will be puffy. Remove from oven; gently press indentations with teaspoon.

6. Return to oven 1 to 2 minutes. Cool cookies in muffin cups 5 minutes. Remove to wire rack; cool completely.

7. Fill each cookie cup with desired fillings. Decorate as desired.                    *Makes 12 cookies*

# FLOURLESS PEANUT BUTTER COOKIES

**1 cup peanut butter**
**1 cup packed light brown sugar**
**1 egg**
**24 milk chocolate candy stars or other solid milk chocolate candy**

Preheat oven to 350°F. Combine peanut butter, sugar and egg in medium bowl; beat until blended and smooth.

Shape dough into 24 balls about 1½ inches in diameter. Place 2 inches apart on ungreased cookie sheets. Press one chocolate star on top of each cookie. Bake 10 to 12 minutes or until set. Transfer to wire racks to cool completely.

*Makes about 2 dozen cookies*

# Express Desserts & Sweets

## APPLE–GINGERBREAD MINI CAKES

**1 large Cortland or Jonathan apple, cored and quartered**
**1 package (14½ ounces) gingerbread cake and**
     **cookie mix**
**1 cup water**
**1 egg**
     **Powdered sugar**

**Microwave Directions**
1. Lightly grease 10 (6- to 7-ounce) custard cups; set aside. Grate apple in food processor or with hand-held grater. Combine grated apple, cake mix, water and egg in medium bowl; stir until well blended. Spoon about ⅓ cup mix into each custard cup, filling cups ½ full.

2. Arrange 5 cups in microwave. Microwave at HIGH 2 minutes. Rotate cups ½ turn. Microwave 1 minute more or until cakes are springy when touched and look slightly moist on top. Cool on wire rack. Repeat with remaining cakes.

3. To unmold cakes, run a small knife around edge of custard cups to loosen cakes while still warm. Invert on cutting board and tap lightly until cake drops out. Place on plates. When cool enough, dust with powdered sugar, if desired. Serve warm or at room temperature. *Makes 10 cakes*

SERVING SUGGESTION: Serve with vanilla ice cream, whipped cream or crème anglaise.

**Prep and Cook Time: 20 minutes**

# CHOCOLATE SPRINKLE ANGEL FOOD CAKE

**1 package DUNCAN HINES® Angel Food Cake Mix
3 tablespoons chocolate sprinkles**

1. Remove top rack from oven; move remaining rack to lowest position. Preheat oven to 350°F.

2. Prepare batter following package directions. Fold in chocolate sprinkles. Pour batter into *ungreased* 10-inch tube pan. Bake and cool following package directions. Garnish as desired.                    *Makes 12 to 16 servings*

# EASY FRESH LEMON ICE CREAM

**2 cups heavy cream or whipping cream or half-and-half
1 cup sugar
   Grated peel of 1 SUNKIST® lemon
⅓ cup fresh squeezed SUNKIST® lemon juice
6 to 10 SUNKIST® lemon boats or shells (see Note, optional)**

In large bowl, combine cream and sugar; stir to dissolve sugar. Blend in lemon peel and juice. (Mixture will thicken slightly.) Pour into shallow pan and freeze until firm, about 4 hours. Serve in lemon boats or shells, or in dessert dishes. Garnish with fresh mint leaves and strawberries, if desired.

*Makes 6 to 9 servings (about 3 cups)*

LEMON AND FRUIT VARIATION: Stir in ½ cup mashed strawberries, bananas or kiwifruit into the slightly thickened lemon mixture before freezing. Makes about 3½ cups.

NOTE: To make lemon boats, cut a large lemon in half lengthwise. Carefully ream out juice (save for use in other recipes). Scrape shells clean with a spoon. If desired, edges may be notched or scalloped. To prevent tipping, cut a thin slice from the bottom of each shell. To make lemon shells, cut lemon half crosswise; proceed as above.

## Quick Tip

For a quick finish, simply dust Chocolate Sprinkle Angel Food Cake with confectioners' sugar.

# EASY CITRUS BERRY SHORTCAKE

**1 individual sponge cake**
**1 tablespoon orange juice**
**¼ cup lemon chiffon sugar-free, nonfat yogurt**
**¼ cup thawed frozen fat-free nondairy whipped topping**
**⅔ cup sliced strawberries or raspberries**

1. Place sponge cake on serving plate. Drizzle with orange juice.

2. Fold together yogurt and whipped topping. Spoon half of mixture onto cake. Top with berries and remaining yogurt mixture. Garnish with mint leaves and orange peel, if desired.

*Makes 1 serving*

# STRAWBERRY CHANTILLY

**1 box (10 ounces) BIRDS EYE® frozen Strawberries**
**1 cup heavy cream***
**2 tablespoons sugar***
**½ teaspoon vanilla extract***
**Belgian waffles or pound cake slices, toasted**

*\*For extra-quick preparation, substitute 2 cups thawed frozen whipped topping for cream, sugar and vanilla.*

• Thaw strawberries according to package directions until partially thawed. Mash strawberries in bowl.

• Beat cream, sugar and vanilla in large bowl until stiff peaks form. Gently fold in ¼ cup mashed strawberries.

• Spoon remaining strawberries over waffles. Top with whipped cream mixture.          *Makes about 4 servings*

**Prep Time:** 20 minutes

## Express Recipe

To make an easy apple crisp, place 2 (15-ounce) cans apple pie filling in a 12×8-inch baking dish. Combine 1¼ cups uncooked quick oats, ½ cup packed brown sugar, ¼ cup all-purpose flour and 1 teaspoon ground cinnamon with ⅓ cup melted butter; mix well. Sprinkle this mixture over the pie filling and bake for 30 minutes in a preheated 375°F oven or until the topping is slightly browned. Serve the apple crisp while it is still warm.

# LUSCIOUS LIME ANGEL FOOD CAKE ROLLS

**1 package (16 ounces) angel food cake mix**
**2 drops green food coloring (optional)**
**2 containers (8 ounces each) lime-flavored nonfat**
   **sugar-free yogurt**

1. Preheat oven to 350°F. Line two 17×11¼×1-inch jelly-roll pans with parchment or waxed paper; set aside.

2. Prepare angel food cake mix according to package directions. Divide batter evenly between prepared pans. Draw knife through batter to remove large air bubbles. Bake 12 minutes or until cakes are lightly browned and toothpick inserted into centers comes out clean.

3. Invert each cake onto separate clean towel. Starting at short end, roll up warm cake, jelly-roll fashion, with towel inside. Cool cakes completely.

4. Place 1 to 2 drops green food coloring in each container of yogurt, if desired; stir well. Unroll cakes; remove towels. Spread each cake with 1 container yogurt, leaving 1-inch border. Roll up cakes; place seam side down. Slice each cake roll into 8 pieces. Garnish with lime slices, if desired. Serve immediately or refrigerate.            *Makes 16 servings*

# THE CHERRY CORDIAL

**HERSHEY'S Double Chocolate Sundae Syrup**
**Cherry vanilla ice cream**
**HERSHEY'S Chocolate Shell Topping**
**REDDI-WIP® Whipped Topping**
**Maraschino cherry**

• Pour layer of HERSHEY'S Double Chocolate Sundae Syrup in shallow ice cream dish.

• Place large scoop of ice cream on top of syrup.

• Shake HERSHEY'S Chocolate Shell Topping according to instructions. Squeeze generous amount over ice cream. Allow to harden for 30 seconds.

• Top with REDDI-WIP Whipped Topping and maraschino cherry.            *Makes 1 sundae*

## GRILLED BANANA SPLIT

**1 large ripe firm banana**
**4 tablespoons chocolate syrup**
**⅔ cup vanilla ice cream**
**2 tablespoons toasted sliced almonds**

1. Prepare grill for direct cooking.

2. Cut unpeeled banana in half lengthwise; brush ½ teaspoon melted butter over cut sides. Grill banana halves, cut side down, over medium-hot coals 2 minutes or until lightly browned; turn. Grill 2 minutes or until tender.

3. Place 1 tablespoon syrup in each of two bowls.

4. Cut banana halves in half crosswise; carefully remove peel. Place 2 pieces banana in each bowl; top with ⅓ cup ice cream, 1 tablespoon chocolate syrup, and 1 tablespoon almonds; serve immediately.          *Makes 2 servings*

## DULCE DE LECHE

**1 (14-ounce) can EAGLE BRAND® Sweetened Condensed Milk (NOT evaporated milk)**
**Assorted dippers, such as cookies, cake, pound cake or angel food cake cubes, banana chunks, orange slices, apple slices and/or strawberries**

1. Preheat oven to 425°F. Pour Eagle Brand into 9-inch pie plate. Cover with foil; place in larger shallow baking pan. Pour hot water into larger pan to depth of 1 inch.

2. Bake 1 hour or until thick and caramel-colored. Beat until smooth. Cool 1 hour. Refrigerate until serving time. Serve as dip with assorted dippers. Store covered in refrigerator for up to 1 week.          *Makes about 1¼ cups dip*

CAUTION: Never heat an unopened can.

**Prep Time :** 5 minutes
**Bake Time:** 1 hour
**Cool Time:** 1 hour

## SPEEDY PINEAPPLE–LIME SORBET

**1 ripe pineapple, cut into cubes (about 4 cups)**
**⅓ cup frozen limeade concentrate, thawed**
**1 to 2 tablespoons fresh lime juice**
**1 teaspoon grated lime peel**

1. Arrange pineapple in single layer on large baking pan; freeze at least 1 hour or until very firm. Use metal spatula to transfer pineapple to resealable plastic freezer food storage bags; freeze up to 1 month.

2. Combine frozen pineapple, limeade, lime juice and lime peel in food processor; process until smooth and fluffy. If pineapple doesn't become smooth and fluffy, let stand 30 minutes to soften slightly; then repeat processing. Garnish as desired. Serve immediately.     *Makes 8 servings*

## CHOCOLATE MACAROON HEATH® PIE

**½ cup (1 stick) butter or margarine, melted**
**3 cups MOUNDS® Sweetened Coconut Flakes**
**2 tablespoons all-purpose flour**
**1⅓ cups (8-ounce package) HEATH® Milk Chocolate Toffee Bits**
**½ gallon chocolate ice cream, softened**

1. Heat oven to 375°F.

2. Combine butter, coconut and flour in medium bowl. Press into 9-inch pie pan.

3. Bake 10 minutes or until edge is light golden brown. Cool completely.

4. Set aside ⅓ cup toffee bits. Combine ice cream and remaining toffee bits. Spread into cooled crust. Sprinkle with ⅓ cup reserved toffee. Freeze at least 5 hours. Remove from freezer about 10 minutes before serving.

*Makes 6 to 8 servings*

---

# Quick Tip

Speedy Pineapple-Lime Sorbet is best when it is served immediately, but it may be made ahead, stored in the freezer, then softened several minutes before being served.

# Quick Tip

Coulis, which is pronounced Koo•LEE, is a term for a thick sauce made by puréeing fruit, as in Poached Pears with Raspberry Coulis, or vegetables, most often tomatoes. Both of these purées should be strained through a sieve to remove seeds.

## POACHED PEARS WITH RASPBERRY COULIS

**2 firm ripe pears, such as Bosc or Anjou, peeled, halved and cored**
**1 cup unsweetened white grape juice or sweet wine, such as Rhine or Riesling**
**1 package (12 ounces) frozen unsweetened raspberries, thawed**
**1 packet aspartame artificial sweetener *or* equivalent of 2 teaspoons sugar**

1. Preheat oven to 350°F. To poach pears, place pears, cut sides down, in shallow ovenproof baking dish large enough to hold pears in one layer. Pour grape juice over pears. Bake 25 to 30 minutes or until pears are tender when pierced with sharp knife, basting with juices in dish every 10 minutes. Let pears stand in juices until cooled to room temperature, occasionally spooning juices over pears. (Pears may be served at room temperature or covered and chilled up to 3 hours before serving.)

2. To prepare coulis, purée thawed raspberries with their juices in food processor or blender. Strain out and discard seeds, pushing firmly on solids to extract juices. Stir in sweetener. Arrange pears on serving plates; top with coulis. Or, spoon coulis onto serving plates and top with pears.

*Makes 4 servings*

**Prep Time:** 12 minutes
**Bake Time:** 25 minutes
**Chill Time:** 45 minutes

## COUNTRY ROAD SUNDAE

**Rocky road or butter pecan ice cream**
**HERSHEY'S Whoppers® Chocolate Malt Syrup**
**REDDI-WIP® Whipped Topping**
**HERSHEY'S Chocolate Shoppe™ Milk Chocolate Sprinkles**

• Place scoop of ice cream in sundae dish.

• Top with HERSHEY'S Whoppers Chocolate Malt Syrup, REDDI-WIP Whipped Topping and HERSHEY'S Chocolate Shoppe Milk Chocolate Sprinkles.     *Makes 1 sundae*

# TRIPLE CHOCOLATE BROWNIE SUNDAE

**1 brownie**
**1 scoop chocolate ice cream**
   **HERSHEY'S Chocolate Shell Topping**
   **REDDI-WIP® Whipped Topping**

• Place brownie on bottom of sundae dish.

• Place ice cream on top of brownie.

• Shake HERSHEY'S Chocolate Shell Topping according to instructions. Squeeze generous amount over ice cream. Allow to harden for 30 seconds.

• Top with REDDI-WIP Whipped Topping.

*Makes 1 sundae*

# EASY RASPBERRY ICE CREAM

**8 ounces (1¾ cups) frozen unsweetened raspberries**
**2 to 3 tablespoons powdered sugar**
**½ cup whipping cream**

1. Place raspberries in food processor fitted with steel blade. Process using on/off pulsing action about 15 seconds or until raspberries resemble coarse crumbs.

2. Add sugar; process using on/off pulsing action until smooth. With processor running, add cream, processing until well blended. Serve immediately.        *Makes 3 servings*

VARIATION: Substitute other fruits such as strawberries for the raspberries.

# FRESH ORANGE ICE CREAM

**1 quart vanilla ice cream, softened**
**Grated peel of 1 SUNKIST® orange**

In bowl, combine ice cream and orange peel. Return to freezer until firm.        *Makes 4 cups*

Sprinkles are now available in a wide range of colors and shapes. They make a quick, colorful topping for frosted cupcakes, cakes and cookies. If they are unavailable at your local supermarket, look for them in specialty food shops or craft stores.

## ANGEL ALMOND CUPCAKES

**1 package DUNCAN HINES® Angel Food Cake Mix**
**1¼ cups water**
**2 teaspoons almond extract**
**1 container DUNCAN HINES® Wild Cherry Vanilla Frosting**

1. Preheat oven to 350°F.

2. Combine cake mix, water and almond extract in large mixing bowl. Beat at low speed with electric mixer until moistened. Beat at medium speed for 1 minute. Line medium muffin pans with paper baking cups. Fill muffin cups two-thirds full. Bake at 350°F for 20 to 25 minutes or until golden brown, cracked and dry on top. Remove from muffin pans. Cool completely. Frost with frosting.

*Makes 30 to 32 cupcakes*

## LEMONY POACHED GOLDEN APPLES

**3 Washington Golden Delicious apples (about 1 pound), cored**
**1½ cups apple juice**
**1½ teaspoons grated lemon peel**
**⅛ teaspoon ground ginger**

Remove peels from top halves of apples. Combine remaining ingredients; bring to boil. Reduce heat and simmer, uncovered, 5 minutes. Place apples in hot apple juice mixture. Cover and simmer about 15 minutes or until apples are tender but still hold their shape; baste and rotate apples frequently. Remove apples with slotted spoon; cut each apple in half and place in individual serving dishes. Strain juice and return to pan. Boil until juice is reduced to 1 cup; serve warm over warm apples.

*Makes 6 servings*

*Favorite recipe from **Washington Apple Commission***

# SPUN SUGAR BERRIES WITH YOGURT CRÈME

**2 cups fresh raspberries***
**1 container (8 ounces) lemon-flavored nonfat yogurt
    with aspartame sweetener**
**1 cup thawed frozen whipped topping**
**3 tablespoons sugar**

*\*Substitute your favorite fresh berries for the fresh raspberries.*

1. Arrange berries in 4 glass dessert dishes.

2. Combine yogurt and whipped topping in medium bowl. (If not using immediately, cover and refrigerate.) Top berries with yogurt mixture.

3. To prepare spun sugar, pour sugar into heavy medium saucepan. Cook over medium-high heat until sugar melts, shaking pan occasionally. *Do not stir.* As sugar begins to melt, reduce heat to low and cook about 10 minutes or until sugar is completely melted and has turned light golden brown.

4. Remove from heat; let stand 1 minute. Coat metal fork with sugar mixture. Drizzle sugar over berries with circular or back and forth motion. Ropes of spun sugar will harden quickly. Garnish as desired. Serve immediately.

*Makes 4 servings*

# EASY HOMEMADE CHOCOLATE ICE CREAM

**1 (14-ounce) can EAGLE BRAND® Sweetened Condensed
    Milk (NOT evaporated milk)**
**⅔ cup chocolate-flavored syrup**
**2 cups (1 pint) whipping cream, whipped (DO NOT use
    non-dairy whipped topping)**

1. In large mixing bowl, combine Eagle Brand and chocolate syrup. Fold in whipped cream. Pour into 9×5-inch loaf pan or other 2-quart container; cover.

2. Freeze 6 hours or until firm. Return leftovers to freezer.

*Makes about 1½ quarts ice cream*

## LIGHT BANANA CREAM PIE

**1 package (1.9 ounces) sugar-free vanilla instant pudding and pie filling (4 servings)**
**2¾ cups low fat milk**
**4 ripe, medium DOLE® Bananas, sliced**
**1 (9-inch) ready-made graham cracker pie crust**
**1 firm, medium DOLE® Banana (optional)**
**Light frozen non-dairy whipped topping, thawed (optional)**

• **Prepare** pudding as directed, using 2¾ cups low fat milk. Stir in 4 sliced ripe bananas.

• **Spoon** banana mixture into pie crust. Place plastic wrap over pie, lightly pressing plastic to completely cover filling. Chill 1 hour or until filling is set. Remove plastic wrap.

• **Cut** firm banana into ½-inch slices. Garnish pie with whipped topping and banana slices.          *Makes 8 servings*

**Prep Time:** 10 minutes
**Chill Time:** 1 hour

## FLUFFY ORANGE PIE

**1 (8-ounce) package cream cheese, softened**
**1 (14-ounce) can sweetened condensed milk**
**1 (6-ounce) can frozen orange juice concentrate, thawed**
**1 cup whipping cream, whipped**
**1 (6-ounce) READY CRUST® Graham Cracker Pie Crust**

1. Beat cream cheese in large bowl with electric mixer until fluffy; gradually beat in sweetened condensed milk, then orange juice concentrate, until smooth. Fold in whipped cream.

2. Pour into crust.

3. Chill 2 hours or until set. Garnish as desired. Refrigerate leftovers.          *Makes 8 servings*

**Preparation Time:** 10 minutes
**Chill Time:** 2 hours

## CHOCOLATE–RUM PARFAITS

**6 to 6½ ounces Mexican chocolate, coarsely chopped\***
**1½ cups whipping cream, divided**
**3 tablespoons golden rum (optional)**
**¾ teaspoon vanilla**
   **Whipped cream, for garnish**
   **Sliced almonds, for garnish**
   **Cookies (optional)**

*\*Or, substitute 6 ounces semisweet chocolate, coarsely chopped,*
*1 tablespoon ground cinnamon and ¼ teaspoon almond extract.*

1. Combine chocolate and 3 tablespoons cream in top of double boiler. Heat over simmering water until smooth, stirring occasionally. Gradually stir in rum, if desired; remove top pan from heat. Let stand at room temperature 15 minutes to cool slightly.

2. Combine remaining cream and vanilla in chilled small bowl. Beat with electric mixer at low speed, then gradually increase speed until stiff peaks form.

3. Gently fold whipped cream into cooled chocolate mixture until uniform in color. Spoon mousse into 4 individual dessert dishes. Refrigerate 2 to 3 hours until firm. Garnish with whipped cream and almonds. Serve with cookies, if desired. *Makes 4 servings*

## APRICOT FOSTER SUNDAE

**1 can (15¼ ounces) DEL MONTE® Apricot Halves**
   **in Heavy Syrup, undrained**
**⅓ cup firmly packed brown sugar**
**2 tablespoons butter or margarine**
**1 pint vanilla ice cream**

1. Drain apricot syrup into small saucepan. Bring to boil. Reduce heat to medium-low; simmer 4 minutes.

2. Stir in brown sugar and butter; cook until thickened, stirring constantly. Add apricots; heat through. Spoon over scoops of vanilla ice cream. *Makes 4 servings*

**Prep and Cook Time:** 7 minutes

---

## Quick Tip

For the best results when beating whipping cream, chill the bowl, beaters and cream first—the cold keeps the fat in the cream solid, thus increasing the volume of the resulting whipped cream. Choose a deep, narrow bowl for this task.

# CITRUS SORBET

**1 can (12 ounces) DOLE® Orange Peach Mango or
Tropical Fruit Frozen Juice Concentrate
1 can (8 ounces) DOLE® Crushed Pineapple or Pineapple
Tidbits, drained
½ cup plain nonfat or low fat yogurt
2½ cups cold water**

• Combine frozen juice concentrate, crushed pineapple and yogurt in blender or food processor container; blend until smooth. Stir in water.

• Pour mixture into container of ice cream maker.* Freeze according to manufacturer's directions.

• Serve sorbet in dessert dishes.          *Makes 10 servings*

*\*Or, pour sorbet mixture into 8-inch square metal pan; cover. Freeze 1½ to 2 hours or until slightly firm. Place in large bowl; beat with electric mixer on medium speed 1 minute or until slushy. Return mixture to metal pan; repeat freezing and beating steps. Freeze until firm, about 6 hours or overnight.*

PASSION–BANANA SORBET: Substitute DOLE® Pine-Orange-Banana Frozen Juice Concentrate for frozen juice concentrate. Prepare sorbet as directed above except reduce water to 2 cups and omit canned pineapple.

**Prep Time:** 20 minutes
**Freeze Time:** 20 minutes

# BAKED APPLES

**2 tablespoons sugar
2 tablespoons GRANDMA'S® Molasses
2 tablespoons raisins, chopped
2 tablespoons chopped walnuts
6 apples, cored**

Heat oven to 350°F. In medium bowl, combine sugar, molasses, raisins and walnuts. Fill apple cavities with molasses mixture. Place in 13×9-inch baking dish. Pour ½ cup hot water over apples and bake 25 minutes or until soft.          *Makes 6 servings*

# FRUIT MEDLEY DESSERT

**1 package (18 ounces) NESTLÉ® TOLL HOUSE®
Refrigerated Sugar Cookie Bar Dough
1 container (32 ounces) lowfat vanilla yogurt *or*
1 quart vanilla frozen yogurt
4 cups fresh fruit (blueberries, raspberries, sliced apples,
cherries, nectarines, peaches and/or strawberries)**

**PREHEAT** oven to 325°F.

**ROLL** chilled dough on floured surface to ¼-inch thickness. Cut out 24 shapes using 3-inch cookie cutters. Place on ungreased baking sheets.

**BAKE** for 10 to 14 minutes or until edges are light golden brown. Cool on baking sheets for 2 minutes; remove to wire racks to cool completely.

**PLACE** two cookies on each plate. Top with ½ cup yogurt and ½ cup fruit mixture. Place third cookie on top.

*Makes 8 servings*

# FRUITFUL FROZEN YOGURT

**1 envelope unflavored gelatin
¼ cup cold water
1½ cups puréed fresh fruit
1 carton (16 ounces) vanilla low-fat yogurt
¼ to ½ cup sugar**

1. Sprinkle gelatin over cold water in small saucepan; let stand 5 minutes to soften. Stir over low heat until gelatin dissolves. Remove from heat. Stir in fruit purée, yogurt and sugar to taste. Pour into 9-inch square pan; freeze until almost firm.

2. Coarsely chop mixture; spoon into chilled bowl. Beat with electric mixer until smooth. Cover; store in freezer.

*Makes 5 servings*

TIP: Dark fruits such as strawberries, raspberries and cherries make this recipe as pleasing to the eye as it is to the palate.

*Favorite recipe from* **Wisconsin Milk Marketing Board**

## Express Recipe

To prepare raspberry brownies, sprinkle a pint of red raspberries into a greased 8×8-inch baking pan. Prepare a 15-ounce brownie mix according to package directions. Pour the batter over the raspberries and bake following the package directions. Cool the brownies and frost with chocolate frosting, if desired.

## ANGEL FOOD CAKE WITH PINEAPPLE SAUCE

**1 can (20 ounces) DOLE® Crushed Pineapple, undrained**
**2 tablespoons sugar**
**1 tablespoon cornstarch**
**1 tablespoon orange marmalade, peach or apricot fruit spread**
**1 prepared angel food cake**

• Combine crushed pineapple with juice, sugar, cornstarch and orange marmalade in small saucepan. Bring to a boil. Reduce heat to low; cook, stirring constantly, 2 minutes or until sauce thickens. Cool slightly. Sauce can be served warm or chilled.

• Cut angel food cake into 12 slices. To serve, spoon sauce over each slice. *Makes 12 servings*

**Prep Time:** 10 minutes
**Cook Time:** 5 minutes

## APPLE YOGURT TRIFLE

**1 Washington Granny Smith apple, cored and finely chopped**
**2 (8-ounce) containers low-fat cherry yogurt**
**10 tablespoons crunchy nutlike cereal nuggets**

Evenly divide half the chopped apple pieces among four parfait dishes or tall glasses. Divide yogurt from one 8-ounce container among dishes. Add 2 tablespoons cereal to each trifle, then top with layers of remaining yogurt, chopped apple and a sprinkle of cereal on top. Refrigerate at least 15 to 20 minutes before serving to allow cereal to soften slightly. *Makes 4 servings*

*Favorite recipe from Washington Apple Commission*

## CAFFÉ EN FORCHETTA

**2 cups reduced-fat (2%) milk**
**1 cup cholesterol-free egg substitute**
**½ cup sugar**
**2 tablespoons no-sugar-added mocha-flavored instant coffee**
**Grated chocolate *or* 6 chocolate-covered coffee beans (optional)**

1. Preheat oven to 325°F.

2. Combine all ingredients except grated chocolate in medium bowl. Whisk until instant coffee has dissolved and mixture is foamy. Pour into 6 individual custard cups. Place cups in 13×9-inch baking pan. Fill pan with hot water halfway up sides of cups.

3. Bake 55 to 60 minutes or until knife inserted halfway between center and edge comes out clean. Serve warm or at room temperature. Garnish with grated chocolate or chocolate-covered coffee beans, if desired.

*Makes 6 servings*

## CHOCOLATE SATIN PIE

**1 *prepared* 9-inch (6 ounces) graham cracker crumb crust**
**1 can (12 fluid ounces) NESTLÉ® CARNATION® Evaporated Milk**
**2 large egg yolks**
**2 cups (12-ounce package) NESTLÉ® TOLL HOUSE® Semi-Sweet Chocolate Morsels**
**Whipped cream (optional)**
**Chopped nuts (optional)**

WHISK together evaporated milk and egg yolks in medium saucepan. Heat over medium-low heat, stirring constantly, until mixture is very hot and thickens slightly; do not boil. Remove from heat; stir in morsels until completely melted and mixture is smooth.

POUR into crust; refrigerate for 3 hours or until firm. Top with whipped cream before serving; sprinkle with nuts.

*Makes 10 servings*

## Quick Tip

Enjoy your dinner coffee a whole new way. Translated from Italian, Caffé en Forchetta literally means "coffee on a fork." However, a spoon is recommended when serving this wonderfully creamy dessert.

# PASSIONATE SORBET

**2 cups MAUNA LA'I® Paradise Passion® Juice Drink**
**¼ cup sugar**
**½ envelope of unflavored gelatin**

1. Combine Mauna La'i Paradise Passion Juice Drink and sugar in medium saucepan. Sprinkle gelatin over juice drink and let sit 1 to 2 minutes to soften. Cook on low heat until gelatin and sugar dissolve, stirring occasionally. Pour into 9×9-inch pan and freeze until just firm.

2. Remove from freezer and cut into small pieces. Place frozen pieces in food processor. Process until light and creamy. Return to pan. Cover and freeze until firm. To serve, scrape off thin layers with spoon.    *Makes 6 servings*

# CHOCOLATE TRIPLE LAYER PIE

**2 cups cold milk**
**2 (4-serving-size) packages chocolate flavor instant**
**    pudding & pie filling**
**1 (6-ounce) READY CRUST® Graham Cracker Pie Crust**
**1 (8-ounce) tub frozen whipped topping, thawed,**
**    divided**

1. Pour milk into large bowl. Add pudding mixes. Beat with wire whisk 1 minute. (Mixture will be thick.) Spoon 1½ cups of the pudding into crust.

2. Gently stir half of whipped topping into remaining pudding. Spread over pudding in crust. Top with remaining whipped topping.

3. Refrigerate 4 hours or until set. Refrigerate leftovers.
*Makes 8 servings*

**Preparation Time:** 15 minutes
**Chilling Time:** 4 hours

# CHOCOLATE ICE CREAM CUPS

**1 (12-ounce) package semi-sweet chocolate chips (2 cups)**
**1 (14-ounce) can EAGLE BRAND® Sweetened Condensed Milk (NOT evaporated milk)**
**1 cup finely ground pecans**
**Ice cream, any flavor**

1. In heavy saucepan over low heat, melt chips with Eagle Brand; remove from heat. Stir in pecans. In individual paper-lined muffin cups, spread about 2 tablespoons chocolate mixture. With lightly greased spoon, spread chocolate on bottom and up side of each cup.

2. Freeze 2 hours or until firm. Before serving, remove paper liners. Fill chocolate cups with ice cream. Store unfilled cups tightly covered in freezer.         *Makes about 1½ dozen cups*

NOTE: It is easier to remove the paper liners if the chocolate cups sit at room temperature for about 5 minutes first.

# PUMPKIN GINGERBREAD SURPRISE

**2 tablespoons butter**
**½ (6¼-ounce) bag miniature marshmallows**
**1 cup gingersnaps**
**1 quart DREYER'S® or EDY'S® Grand Pumpkin Ice Cream***
**Pumpkin pie spice or ground nutmeg**

*\*Available September through November.*

• Melt butter in saucepan over low heat; slowly add marshmallows, stirring constantly until melted.

• Divide gingersnaps among 4 serving bowls or dessert plates; top each serving with 1 scoop DREYER'S® or EDY'S® Grand Pumpkin Ice Cream.

• Spoon marshmallow mixture over ice cream; sprinkle with pumpkin pie spice.         *Makes 4 servings*

## RICH CHOCOLATE MOUSSE

**1 cup (6 ounces) NESTLÉ® TOLL HOUSE® Semi-Sweet Chocolate Morsels**
**3 tablespoons butter, cut into pieces**
**2 teaspoons TASTER'S CHOICE® 100% Pure Instant Coffee**
**1 tablespoon hot water**
**2 teaspoons vanilla extract**
**½ cup heavy whipping cream**

**MICROWAVE** morsels and butter in medium, uncovered, microwave-safe bowl on HIGH (100%) power for 1 minute. STIR. Morsels may retain some of their original shape. If necessary, microwave at additional 10- to 15-second intervals, stirring just until morsels are melted. Dissolve Taster's Choice in hot water; stir into chocolate. Stir in vanilla extract; cool to room temperature.

**WHIP** cream in small mixer bowl on high speed until stiff peaks form; fold into chocolate mixture. Spoon into tall glasses; refrigerate for 1 hour or until set. Garnish as desired.

*Makes 2 servings*

## STRAWBERRIES WITH HONEYED YOGURT SAUCE

**1 quart fresh strawberries**
**1 cup plain low-fat yogurt**
**1 tablespoon orange juice**
**1 to 2 teaspoons honey**
**⅛ teaspoon ground cinnamon (optional)**

Rinse and hull strawberries. Combine yogurt, juice, honey and cinnamon, if desired, in small bowl; mix well. Serve sauce over strawberries.

*Makes 4 servings*

---

# Express Recipe

You can quickly prepare a showy dessert early in the day to serve for dinner. Simply beat 2 (8-ounce) packages of reduced-fat cream cheese, 2 tablespoons milk, 3 tablespoons sugar and ¼ teaspoon almond extract in a medium bowl with an electric mixer at medium speed until the mixture is well blended. Place a vanilla wafer in the bottom of each of 8 (4-ounce) custard cups. Arrange another 4 wafers around the side of each cup, then fill the cups with the cream cheese mixture. Top each cup with ¼ cup of cherry pie filling. Cover and chill for 6 to 8 hours.

## CUPID CAKES

**1 package (10 ounces) frozen strawberries, thawed**
**½ cup whipping cream, whipped**
**2 frozen all-butter pound cakes (10¾ ounces each),**
    **thawed**
**½ cup strawberry or seedless raspberry preserves**

1. Drain strawberries, reserving 1 tablespoon juice. Discard remaining juice. Gently combine strawberries, reserved juice and 1 tablespoon powdered sugar with whipped cream; set aside.

2. Cut each cake into 12 slices. Spread 12 slices with about 1½ teaspoons preserves each. Top with remaining slices to make sandwiches, pressing gently to spread preserves to edges. Scrape excess preserves from edges. Place onto serving plates; top with whipped cream mixture.

*Makes 12 servings*

**Prep and Cook Time:** 15 minutes

## HOME IN THE HIGHLANDS SUNDAE

**3 round shortbread butter cookies**
**1 large scoop vanilla ice cream**
  **HEATH® Sundae Syrup**
  **REDDI-WIP® Whipped Topping**

• Place cookies on plate with centers touching.

• Place ice cream over cookies.

• Squeeze generous portion of HEATH Sundae Syrup over ice cream.

• Top generously with REDDI-WIP Whipped Topping.

*Makes 1 sundae*

---

*Express Recipe*

Combine canned cream of coconut and sliced strawberries for a delicious and easy topping for pound cake or angel food cake.

## BANANA CREAM PARFAITS

**1 package (4-serving size) vanilla pudding and pie
filling mix
2 cups low-fat (1%) milk
1 cup coarsely crushed chocolate cookies
2 large ripe bananas, peeled and sliced**

1. Prepare pudding according to package directions, using
low-fat milk; cool 10 minutes, stirring occasionally.

2. In each of 4 parfait or wine glasses, layer 2 tablespoons
cookie crumbs, ¼ cup banana slices and ¼ cup pudding.
Repeat layers. Cover; chill at least 1 hour or up to 6 hours
before serving. Garnish with mint sprigs, if desired.

*Makes 4 servings*

VARIATION: Chocolate pudding and pie filling mix may
be substituted for the vanilla pudding and crushed vanilla
wafers for the chocolate cookies.

**Prep Time:** 20 minutes
**Cook Time:** 5 minutes
**Chill Time:** at least 1 hour

## PETER PAN'S CLOUD DESSERT

**½ cup PETER PAN® Smart Choice Creamy Peanut Butter,
Creamy or Chunky
2 (4-ounce) containers SWISS MISS® Fat Free Vanilla
Pudding
3 cups reduced fat nondairy whipped topping
Chopped peanuts (optional)**

1. In medium bowl, combine Peter Pan Peanut Butter and
pudding; fold in whipped topping.

2. Divide evenly into dessert cups and garnish with peanuts.

3. Refrigerate until chilled.     *Makes 8 servings*

# LUSCIOUS CHOCOLATE COVERED STRAWBERRIES

**3 squares (1 ounce each) semi-sweet chocolate**
**2 tablespoons I CAN'T BELIEVE IT'S NOT BUTTER!®**
**  Spread**
**1 tablespoon coffee liqueur (optional)**
**6 to 8 large strawberries with stems**

In small microwave-safe bowl, microwave chocolate and
I Can't Believe It's Not Butter!® Spread at HIGH (Full Power)
1 minute or until chocolate is melted; stir until smooth. Stir
in liqueur. Dip strawberries in chocolate mixture, then
refrigerate on waxed paper-lined baking sheet until chocolate
is set, at least 1 hour.                    *Makes 6 to 8 strawberries*

# CHERRY DREAM

**5 cups loosely packed angel food cake cubes (about**
**      10 ounces or ½ of large angel food cake)**
**1 (21-ounce) can cherry pie filling**
**1¾ cups (4 ounces) frozen non-dairy whipped topping,**
**    thawed**
**Fresh mint, for garnish**

Sprinkle cake cubes in bottom of 9-inch square baking pan.
Fold cherry pie filling into whipped topping in medium
bowl. Spoon cherry mixture evenly over cake cubes. Let chill,
covered, several hours or overnight. Garnish each serving
with sprig of mint.                          *Makes 8 servings*

*Favorite recipe from **Cherry Marketing Institute***

## Quick Tip

For best results when
covering strawberries
with chocolate,
always allow the
strawberries to dry
completely before
coating them with
the melted chocolate.
Dip the berries into
the chocolate, then
allow the excess
chocolate to drain
off. These decadent
berries are best eaten
the day they are
prepared.

## Express Recipe

Make an easy version of the traditional southern favorite, Banana Pudding. Prepare 1 (4-serving size) package of vanilla or banana-flavored instant pudding mix according to the package directions, then stir in 1½ cups thawed frozen whipped topping. Layer this mixture in a 2-quart casserole dish with 3 dozen vanilla wafers and 3 bananas, cut into slices, beginning with the wafers (repeat the layers one or two times). Garnish with additional whipped topping, if desired, and chill until ready to serve.

# HOT FUDGE WAFFLE SUNDAES

**12 frozen mini-waffles**
**2 tablespoons hot fudge sauce**
**¾ cup Neapolitan ice cream**
**4 tablespoons aerosol light whipped cream**
**Colored sprinkles (optional)**

1. Heat waffles in toaster until lightly browned. Heat hot fudge sauce in microwave according to manufacturer's directions.

2. Arrange three waffles on each of four serving plates. Top with 1 tablespoon of each ice cream flavor. Evenly drizzle hot fudge sauce over top; garnish with whipped cream and sprinkles, if desired.

*Makes 4 servings (3 mini-waffles each)*

# CHOCOLATE PEANUT BUTTER PIE

**1 (14-ounce) can sweetened condensed milk**
**¼ cup creamy peanut butter**
**2 tablespoons unsweetened cocoa powder**
**1 (8-ounce) container frozen whipped topping, thawed**
**1 (6-ounce) chocolate cookie crumb crust**

1. Beat condensed milk, peanut butter and cocoa in large bowl until smooth. Fold in whipped topping. Pour into crust.

2. Freeze at least 6 hours or overnight. Garnish as desired.

*Makes 8 servings*

**Prep Time:** 5 minutes
**Freezing Time:** 6 hours

## Quick Tip

Instead of crushing the gingersnaps, serve them whole with the Peaches & Cream Gingersnap Cups.

## PEACHES & CREAM GINGERSNAP CUPS

**1½ tablespoons gingersnap crumbs (2 cookies)**
**¼ teaspoon ground ginger**
**2 ounces reduced-fat cream cheese, softened**
**1 container (6 ounces) peach yogurt**
**¼ teaspoon vanilla**
**⅓ cup chopped fresh peach or drained canned peach slices in juice**

1. Combine gingersnap crumbs and ginger in small bowl; set aside.

2. Beat cream cheese in small bowl at medium speed of electric mixer until smooth. Add yogurt and vanilla. Beat at low speed until smooth and well blended. Stir in chopped peach.

3. Divide peach mixture between two 6-ounce custard cups. Cover and refrigerate 1 hour. Top each serving with half of gingersnap crumb mixture just before serving. Garnish as desired.     *Makes 2 servings*

## QUICK CHOCOLATE MOUSSE

**1 (14-ounce) can EAGLE BRAND® Sweetened Condensed Milk (NOT evaporated milk)**
**1 (4-serving-size) package instant chocolate pudding and pie filling mix**
**1 cup cold water**
**1 cup (½ pint) whipping cream, whipped**

1. In large mixing bowl, beat Eagle Brand, pudding mix and water; chill 5 minutes.

2. Fold in whipped cream. Spoon into serving dishes; chill. Garnish as desired.     *Makes 8 to 10 servings*

**Prep Time:** 5 minutes

# THE WILD BERRY SUNDAE

**Blueberries, raspberries, blackberries and/or
  strawberries, rinsed and patted dry
Scoops of vanilla ice cream
HERSHEY'S Chocolate Shoppe™ Hot Fudge Topping
REDDI-WIP® Whipped Topping**

• Alternate layers of berries with ice cream and HERSHEY'S Chocolate Shoppe Hot Fudge topping in sundae dish.

• Top with REDDI-WIP Whipped Topping.

*Makes 1 sundae*

# MANGO–PEACH FROZEN YOGURT

**2 medium (8 ounces each) ripe mangoes, peeled
  and cubed
2 cups peach low-fat yogurt
½ cup honey**

In blender or food processor container, process mango cubes until smooth. Add yogurt and honey; process until well combined. Transfer mixture to ice cream maker; freeze according to manufacturer's directions.    *Makes 6 servings*

*Favorite recipe from **National Honey Board***

# PUDDING IN A CLOUD DESSERT

**2 (4-ounce) containers SWISS MISS® Vanilla Pudding
3 cups reduced-fat non-dairy whipped topping
  Fresh mint leaves (optional)**

In medium bowl, fold together pudding and whipped topping. Divide evenly into dessert cups. Refrigerate until chilled. Garnish with mint leaves, if desired.

*Makes 8 (½-cup) servings*

**Preparation Time:** 10 minutes

**Express Recipe**

Waffles are a great dessert, especially when they are paired with special ice cream flavors like rum raisin, Irish cream, bananas foster, coffee or mint chocolate chip. Top with your favorite ice cream topping.

# MANGO COCONUT TROPICAL FREEZE

**1 jar (26 ounces) refrigerated mango slices, drained (or the flesh of 3 ripe mangoes, peeled and cut to equal about 3⅓ cups)**
**½ cup canned cream of coconut**
**1 tablespoon lime juice**
**⅓ cup toasted chopped pecans**

1. Place mango, coconut cream and lime juice in food processor; process 1 to 2 minutes or until smooth.

2. Spoon into small dessert cups or custard cups. Top with pecans. Place cups on pie plate, cover tightly. Freeze 8 hours or overnight. Remove from freezer and allow to thaw slightly before serving. Serve immediately.     *Makes 4 servings*

**Make-Ahead Time:** up to 1 day before serving
**Final Prep Time:** about 30 minutes

# PEACH PARFAIT PIE

**½ cup boiling water**
**1 (3 ounce) package peach flavored gelatin**
**1 pint vanilla ice cream, softened**
**2 cups sliced fresh peaches**
**1 (6-ounce) READY CRUST® Shortbread Pie Crust**

1. Pour boiling water over peach gelatin in medium bowl; stir until gelatin dissolves.

2. Add ice cream; stir until smooth. Fold in peaches. Pour into crust.

3. Freeze until set, about 3 hours. Freeze leftovers.
*Makes 8 servings*

**Prep Time:** 10 minutes
**Freezing Time:** 3 hours

# CHERRY–BERRY CRUMBLE

**1 (21-ounce) can cherry pie filling**
**2 cups fresh or frozen raspberries**
**1 (14-ounce) can EAGLE BRAND® Sweetened Condensed**
**Milk (NOT evaporated milk)**
**1½ cups granola**

1. In medium saucepan over medium heat, cook and stir cherry pie filling and raspberries until heated through. Stir in Eagle Brand; cook and stir 1 minute.

2. Spoon into 2-quart square baking dish or 6 individual dessert dishes. Sprinkle with granola. Serve warm.

*Makes 6 servings*

PEACH–BERRY CRUMBLE: Substitute peach pie filling for cherry pie filling.

CHERRY–RHUBARB CRUMBLE: Substitute fresh or frozen sliced rhubarb for raspberries. In medium saucepan over medium-high heat, cook and stir pie filling and rhubarb until bubbly. Cook and stir 5 minutes more. Proceed as directed above.

**Prep Time: 10 minutes**

# CHOCOLATE MARBLE ANGEL FOOD CAKE

**1 package DUNCAN HINES® Angel Food Cake Mix**
**3 tablespoons chocolate syrup**

1. Remove top rack from oven; move remaining rack to lowest position. Preheat oven to 350°F.

2. Prepare batter following package directions for basic recipe. Remove half the batter to another bowl; set aside. Add chocolate syrup to remaining batter. Fold gently until blended. Alternate large spoonfuls of white and chocolate batters in ungreased 10-inch tube pan. Bake and cool following package directions. *Makes 12 to 16 servings*

TIP: Serve slices drizzled with chocolate syrup for extra chocolate flavor.

---

## Quick Tip

Granola is an easy topping for this Cherry-Berry Crumble. You can also sprinkle it over ice cream. Or, top a mixture of sliced strawberries and vanilla yogurt with your favorite granola.

# SMUCKER'S® ENGLISH BERRY PUDDING

**1 cup SMUCKER'S® Red Raspberry Preserves**
**12 to 16 slices of white bread, crusts removed,**
**cut into half or quarter triangles**
**2 cups *each* raspberries, blueberries and sliced**
**strawberries (fresh or frozen)**

Line deep 1½- to 2-quart bowl with plastic wrap. Line bottom and side of bowl with half of bread triangles. Completely cover surface so no gaps remain between bread slices.

Heat SMUCKER'S® Raspberry Preserves and 6 cups mixed berries in saucepan over high heat. Bring to a boil and simmer 5 minutes to release juices. Spoon half of berry mixture into bread-lined bowl. Cover with half of remaining bread triangles and remaining berry mixture. Cover second layer of berries with remaining bread. Use more bread if needed to completely seal bowl. Cover pudding with plastic wrap.

Place plate over bowl to weigh it down. Refrigerate pudding 12 to 24 hours before serving.

To serve, remove plate and plastic wrap. Unmold bowl onto serving plate. Remove bowl and carefully peel plastic wrap from pudding. Serve pudding dusted with powdered sugar, whipped cream, frozen yogurt or whipped topping.

*Makes 8 servings*

# GRAHAM CRACKER PUDDING

**3 packages (4-serving size each) vanilla-flavored**
**pudding mix (not instant), plus ingredients**
**to prepare**
**1 package (15 ounces) graham cracker crumbs**
**1½ cups light brown sugar, divided**
**3 large bananas, divided**

1. Prepare pudding mixes according to package directions.

2. Sprinkle ⅓ of cracker crumbs on bottom of 13×9-inch baking pan. Sprinkle ½ cup brown sugar over crumbs. Slice 1 banana over brown sugar. Spread half of pudding over bananas. Repeat layers twice, using remaining ingredients. Refrigerate until ready to serve. *Makes 12 to 14 servings*

# Fast Snacks & Beverages

## Express Recipe

With just two ingredients you can make a tasty snack. Coarsely grate Parmesan cheese to measure 2 cups. Place heaping teaspoons of cheese 2 inches apart on a nonstick baking sheet and flatten slightly. Sprinkle with black pepper. Bake in a preheated 450°F oven for 15 to 20 minutes. Cool slightly before removing the crisps from the baking sheet.

## SPARKLING STRAWBERRY–LIME SHAKES

**2 cups (10 ounces) frozen whole unsweetened strawberries**
**1¼ cups lime-flavored sparkling water, divided**
**¼ cup whipping cream or half-and-half**
**1 tablespoon sugar substitute**
**Lime wedges or slices**

1. Place strawberries in blender container; allow to thaw 5 minutes before proceeding. Add 1 cup sparkling water, cream and sugar substitute. Cover; blend until smooth, scraping down side of blender once or twice (mixture will be thick).

2. Gently stir in remaining sparkling water; pour into 2 glasses. Garnish with lime wedges.    *Makes 2 servings*

VARIATIONS: For a tropical variation, add 1 teaspoon banana extract and/or ½ teaspoon coconut extract along with the cream. For a rum-flavored drink add ½ teaspoon rum extract.

TIP: For quick shakes anytime, wash, hull and freeze whole strawberries in a tightly covered container.

# GOLDEN CHICKEN NUGGETS

**1 pound boneless skinless chicken, cut into
1½-inch pieces
¼ cup *French's®* Sweet & Tangy Honey Mustard
2 cups *French's®* French Fried Onions, finely crushed**

1. Preheat oven to 400°F. Toss chicken with mustard in medium bowl.

2. Place French Fried Onions into resealable plastic food storage bag. Toss chicken in onions, a few pieces at a time, pressing gently to adhere.

3. Place nuggets in shallow baking pan. Bake 15 minutes or until chicken is no longer pink in center. Serve with additional honey mustard.    *Makes 4 servings*

**Prep Time:** 5 minutes
**Cook Time:** 15 minutes

# CARAMELIZED NUTS

**1 cup slivered almonds, pecans or walnuts
⅓ cup sugar
½ teaspoon ground cinnamon (optional)
¼ teaspoon grated nutmeg (optional)**

1. To toast nuts, cook and stir in medium skillet over medium heat 9 to 12 minutes until light golden brown. Transfer to small bowl.

2. Sprinkle sugar evenly over bottom of skillet. Cook, without stirring, 2 to 4 minutes until sugar is melted. Remove from heat.

3. Quickly add nuts to skillet; sprinkle with cinnamon and nutmeg, if desired. Return to heat; stir until nuts are coated with melted sugar mixture. Transfer to plate; cool completely.

4. Place nuts on cutting board; coarsely chop. Store in airtight container up to 2 weeks.    *Makes 1 cup nuts*

NOTE: Care should be taken when caramelizing sugar because melted sugar can cause serious burns if spilled or splattered.

---

## Express Recipe

For colorful kabobs, thread cocktail-size smoked sausages, cherry tomatoes, pimiento-stuffed green olives and yellow or orange bell pepper squares onto 8-inch wooden skewers that have been soaked in water for 20 minutes. Place the kabobs on a rack in a shallow baking pan and brush lightly with melted butter. Bake kabobs in a preheated 450°F oven for 4 to 6 minutes or until they are hot.

## QUICK S'MORES

**1 whole graham cracker**
**1 large marshmallow**
**1 teaspoon hot fudge sauce**

1. Break graham cracker in half crosswise. Place one half on small paper plate or microwavable plate; top with marshmallow.

2. Spread remaining ½ of cracker with fudge sauce.

3. Place cracker with marshmallow in microwave. Microwave at HIGH 12 to 14 seconds or until marshmallow puffs up. Immediately place remaining cracker, fudge side down, over marshmallow. Press crackers gently to even out marshmallow layer. Cool completely.                    *Makes 1 serving*

## BLUE'S CHILLIN' BANANA COOLERS

**2 ripe medium bananas, peeled**
**4 flat wooden ice cream sticks**
**½ cup "M&M's"® Chocolate Mini Baking Bits**
**⅓ cup hot fudge ice cream topping, at room temperature**

Line baking sheet with waxed paper; set aside. Cut each banana in half crosswise. Insert wooden stick about 1½ inches into center of cut end of each banana. Place on prepared baking sheet; freeze until firm, at least 2 hours. Place "M&M's"® Chocolate Mini Baking Bits in shallow dish. Place fudge sauce in separate shallow dish. Working with 1 banana at a time, place frozen banana in fudge sauce; turn banana and spread fudge sauce evenly onto banana with small rubber scraper. Immediately place banana on plate with "M&M's"® Chocolate Mini Baking Bits; turn to coat lightly. Return to baking sheet in freezer. Repeat with remaining bananas. Freeze until fudge sauce is very firm, at least 2 hours. Let stand 5 minutes before serving. Store tightly covered in freezer.                    *Makes 4 servings*

---

# Quick Tip

S'mores can be made the night before and wrapped in plastic wrap or sealed in a small plastic food storage bag. Store at room temperature until ready to pack in your child's lunch box the next morning.

# ICED CAPPUCCINO

**1 cup fat-free vanilla frozen yogurt or fat-free vanilla
    ice cream**
**1 cup cold strong-brewed coffee**
**1 teaspoon unsweetened cocoa powder**
**1 teaspoon vanilla**
**1 packet sugar substitute *or* equivalent of
    2 teaspoons sugar**

1. Place all ingredients in food processor or blender; process until smooth. Place container in freezer; freeze 1½ to 2 hours or until top and sides of mixture are partially frozen.

2. Scrape sides of container; process until smooth and frothy. Garnish as desired. Serve immediately.      *Makes 2 servings*

TIP: To add an extra flavor boost to this refreshing drink, add orange peel, lemon peel or a dash of ground cinnamon to your coffee grounds before brewing.

# BANANA S'MORES

**1 firm DOLE® Banana, sliced**
**12 graham cracker squares**
**6 large marshmallows**
**1 bar (1.55 ounces) milk chocolate candy**

**Microwave Directions**
• Arrange 4 banana slices on each of 6 graham cracker squares. Top with marshmallow. Microwave on HIGH 12 to 15 seconds or until puffed.

• Place 2 squares chocolate on remaining 6 graham crackers. Microwave on HIGH 1 minute or until just soft. Put halves together to make sandwich.      *Makes 6 servings*

**Prep Time:** 5 minutes
**Cook Time:** 1 minute

# PEPPERONI–OREGANO FOCACCIA

**1 tablespoon cornmeal**
**1 package (10 ounces) refrigerated pizza crust dough**
**½ cup finely chopped pepperoni (3 to 3½ ounces)**
**1½ teaspoons finely chopped fresh oregano leaves**
    ***or* ½ teaspoon dried oregano leaves**
**2 teaspoons olive oil**

Preheat oven to 425°F. Grease large baking sheet, then sprinkle sheet with cornmeal; set aside.

Unroll dough onto lightly floured surface. Pat dough into 12×9-inch rectangle. Sprinkle half the pepperoni and half the oregano over one side of dough. Fold over dough making 6×4½-inch rectangle.

Roll dough into 12×9-inch rectangle. Place on prepared baking sheet. Prick dough with fork at 2-inch intervals, about 30 times. Brush with oil; sprinkle with remaining pepperoni and oregano.

Bake 12 to 15 minutes until golden brown. (Prick dough several more times if dough puffs as it bakes.) Cut into squares.

*Makes 12 servings*

# MARSHMALLOW CHOCOLATE SHAKE

**2 cups fat free vanilla ice cream**
**¾ cup nonfat milk**
**⅓ cup SWISS MISS® Fat Free Hot Cocoa Mix with Mini Marshmallows**
**⅛ teaspoon almond extract (optional)**

1. Combine *all* ingredients in blender; blend until smooth.

*Makes 3 (6-ounce) servings*

## Express Recipe

For a fun snack, dip pretzel rods into melted chocolate. Melt 1 (6-ounce) bag of semisweet, milk or white chocolate chips in a microwavable bowl at HIGH for 1 to 1½ minutes, stirring frequently. Dip half of each pretzel rod into the melted chocolate, allowing the excess to run off. Coat the chocolate with sprinkles, colored sugar, coconut or finely chopped nuts. Place them on cooling racks and allow them to dry completely.

# CHERRY-BERRY SMOOTHIE

**1 cup frozen whole unsweetened pitted dark
    sweet cherries**
**1 cup frozen whole unsweetened strawberries**
**1 cup cranberry-cherry juice**

In blender, purée frozen pitted dark sweet cherries, frozen strawberries and juice, stirring as needed, until smooth.

*Makes 1 (16-ounce) serving*

NOTE: Frozen pitted dark sweet cherries may be replaced with ¾ cup well-drained canned pitted dark sweet cherries and four ice cubes.

*Favorite recipe from **National Cherry Growers***

# FROZEN FUDGE POPS

**½ cup nonfat sweetened condensed milk**
**¼ cup unsweetened cocoa powder**
**1¼ cups nonfat evaporated milk**
**1 teaspoon vanilla**

1. Beat together sweetened condensed milk and cocoa in medium bowl. Add evaporated milk and vanilla; beat until smooth.

2. Pour mixture into 8 small paper cups or 8 popsicle molds. Freeze about 2 hours or until beginning to set. Insert wooden popsicle sticks; freeze until solid.          *Makes 8 servings*

# HERBAL CRANBERRY PUNCH

**2½ cups cranberry juice cocktail**
**2½ cups water**
**4 orange, apple or raspberry herbal tea bags**
**2 to 3 tablespoons sugar (optional)**

Combine cranberry juice and water in medium saucepan. Bring to a boil over medium heat. Add tea bags, remove from heat; cover. Let steep at least 5 minutes. Remove tea bags and discard. Add sugar, if desired.          *Makes 6 servings*

## ORIGINAL RANCH® OYSTER CRACKERS

**1 box (16 ounces) oyster crackers**
**¼ cup vegetable oil**
**1 packet (1 ounce) HIDDEN VALLEY® The Original Ranch®**
**Salad Dressing & Seasoning Mix**

Place crackers in a gallon size Glad® Fresh Protection Bag. Pour oil over crackers and toss to coat. Add salad dressing mix; toss again until coated. Spread evenly on large baking sheet. Bake at 250°F for 15 to 20 minutes.  *Makes 8 cups*

## ORIGINAL RANCH® SNACK MIX

**8 cups KELLOGG'S® CRISPIX® cereal**
**2½ cups small pretzels**
**2½ cups bite-size Cheddar cheese crackers (optional)**
**3 tablespoons vegetable oil**
**1 packet (1 ounce) HIDDEN VALLEY® The Original Ranch®**
**Salad Dressing & Seasoning Mix**

Combine cereal, pretzels and crackers in a gallon-size Glad® Zipper Storage Bag. Pour oil over mixture. Seal bag and toss to coat. Add salad dressing & seasoning mix; seal bag and toss again until coated.  *Makes 10 cups*

---

## Express Recipe

For an easy sweet treat, divide 1 package (6-count) refrigerated bread sticks into 6 pieces and roll each piece into a 12-inch rope. Roll each rope in a mixture of 2 tablespoons sugar and ½ teaspoon ground cinnamon. Twist ropes into pretzel shapes and place them on a greased baking sheet. Bake in a preheated 350°F oven for 15 to 18 minutes or until lightly browned. Cool 5 minutes before serving them.

## Quick Tip

To make a quick dip, place 4 ounces of reduced-fat cream cheese, 1 cup of sour cream, 2 to 3 tablespoons milk, ½ teaspoon vanilla and ¼ teaspoon ground nutmeg in a blender. Process until the mixture is smooth. Serve with banana slices, sliced strawberries or apple slices.

# FANTASY CINNAMON APPLEWICHES

**4 slices raisin bread**
**⅓ cup reduced-fat cream cheese**
**¼ cup finely chopped unpeeled apple**
**⅛ teaspoon ground cinnamon**

1. Toast bread. Cut into desired shapes using large cookie cutters.

2. Combine cream cheese and apple in small bowl; spread onto toast.

3. Combine 1 teaspoon sugar and cinnamon in another small bowl; sprinkle evenly over cream cheese mixture.

*Makes 4 servings*

# CAFÉ FRAPPE

**2 tablespoons instant coffee**
**¾ cup warm water**
**1 (14-ounce) can EAGLE BRAND® Sweetened Condensed Milk (NOT evaporated milk)**
**1 teaspoon vanilla extract**
**4 cups ice cubes**

1. In small mixing bowl, dissolve coffee in water. In blender container, combine dissolved coffee, Eagle Brand and vanilla; blend well.

2. Gradually add ice, blending until smooth. Serve immediately. Refrigerate leftovers.     *Makes 4 servings*

## ORANGE ICED TEA

**2 SUNKIST® oranges**
**4 cups boiling water**
**5 tea bags**
  **Ice cubes**
  **Honey or brown sugar to taste**

With vegetable peeler, peel each orange in continuous spiral, removing only outer colored layer of peel (eat peeled fruit or save for other uses). In large pitcher, pour boiling water over tea bags and orange peel. Cover and steep 5 minutes. Remove tea bags; chill tea mixture with peel in covered container. To serve, remove peel and pour over ice cubes in tall glasses. Sweeten to taste with honey. Garnish with orange quarter-cartwheel slices and fresh mint leaves, if desired.

*Makes 4 (8-ounce) servings*

## LEMON HERBAL ICED TEA

**2 SUNKIST® lemons**
**4 cups boiling water**
**6 herbal tea bags (peppermint and spearmint blend**
  **or ginger-flavored)**
  **Ice cubes**
  **Honey or sugar to taste**

With vegetable peeler, peel each lemon in continuous spiral, removing only outer colored layer of peel (save peeled fruit for other uses). In large pitcher, pour boiling water over tea bags and lemon peel. Cover and steep 10 minutes. Remove tea bags; chill tea mixture with peel in covered container. To serve, remove peel and pour over ice cubes in tall glasses. Sweeten to taste with honey. Garnish with lemon half-cartwheel slices, if desired.

*Makes 4 (8-ounce) servings*

## SUPER NACHOS

**12 large baked low-fat tortilla chips (about 1½ ounces)**
**½ cup (2 ounces) shredded reduced-fat Cheddar cheese**
**¼ cup fat-free refried beans**
**2 tablespoons chunky salsa**

1. Arrange chips in single layer on large microwavable plate. Sprinkle cheese evenly over chips.

2. Spoon teaspoonfuls of beans over chips; top with ½ teaspoonfuls of salsa.

3. Microwave at MEDIUM (50%) 1½ minutes; rotate dish. Microwave 1 to 1½ minutes or until cheese is melted.

*Makes 2 servings*

CONVENTIONAL DIRECTIONS: Substitute foil-covered baking sheet for microwavable plate. Assemble nachos as directed on prepared baking sheet. Bake at 350°F for 10 to 12 minutes or until cheese is melted.

## CREAMY CHOCOLATE DIPPED STRAWBERRIES

**1 cup HERSHEY'S Semi-Sweet Chocolate Chips**
**½ cup HERSHEY'S Premier White Chips**
**1 tablespoon shortening (do *not* use butter, margarine, spread or oil)**
**Fresh strawberries, rinsed and patted dry (about 2 pints)**

1. Line tray with wax paper.

2. Place chocolate chips, white chips and shortening in medium microwave-safe bowl. Microwave at HIGH (100%) 1 minute; stir. If necessary, microwave at HIGH an additional 15 seconds at a time, stirring after each heating, just until chips are melted when stirred. Holding top, dip bottom two-thirds of each strawberry into melted mixture; shake gently to remove excess. Place on prepared tray.

3. Refrigerate about 1 hour or until coating is firm. Cover; refrigerate leftover dipped berries. For best results, use within 24 hours.

*Makes about 3 dozen dipped berries*

---

# Quick Tip

For a single serving of Super Nachos, arrange 6 large tortilla chips on a microwavable plate; top them with ¼ cup cheese, 2 tablespoons refried beans and 1 tablespoon salsa. Microwave at MEDIUM (50%) 1 minute; rotate the plate. Continue to microwave 30 seconds to 1 minute or until the cheese is melted.

# KALEIDOSCOPE HONEY POPS

**2¼ cups water**
**¾ cup honey**
**3 cups assorted fruit, cut into small pieces**
**12 (3-ounce) paper cups or popsicle molds**
**12 popsicle sticks**

Whisk together water and honey in pitcher until well blended. Place ¼ cup fruit in each mold. Divide honey mixture between cups. Freeze about 1 hour or until partially frozen. Insert popsicle sticks; freeze until firm and ready to serve. *Makes 12 servings*

*Favorite recipe from* **National Honey Board**

# PIÑA COLADA MILKSHAKE

**2 cups (1 pint) coconut sorbet**
**2 cups (1 pint) vanilla frozen yogurt or ice cream**
**¾ cup pineapple juice**
**¼ cup dark rum (optional)**

Combine all ingredients in blender. Blend until smooth.
*Makes 4 servings*

# SWISS BERRY FREEZE

**2 cups unsweetened frozen raspberries**
**2 cups fat free milk**
**2 (1¼-ounce) envelopes SWISS MISS® Premiere Chocolate Raspberry Truffle Cocoa Mix**

1. Combine *all* ingredients in blender; blend until smooth. Add ice if desired; blend. *Makes 3 (9-ounce) servings*

## Express Recipe

Combine ½ cup low-fat small curd cottage cheese and ½ cup creamy peanut butter in a blender. Process until the mixture is smooth. Stir in ½ cup drained canned crushed pineapple until well blended. Spread this mixture into 12 (3-inch-long) celery sticks or serve with apple slices.

# SPICED NUTS

**1 egg white**
**2 tablespoons sugar**
**1 teaspoon ground cinnamon**
**½ teaspoon ground allspice**
**1¾ cups pecan halves**

1. Preheat oven to 325°F. Grease baking sheet; set aside.

2. Beat egg white in small bowl with electric mixer until soft peaks form. Beat in sugar, cinnamon and allspice. Stir in pecans until coated.

3. Spread pecans on prepared baking sheet, separating pecans. Bake about 12 minutes or until crisp. Let stand until cooled.

*Makes about ¼ pound*

# PARADISE FREEZE

**1 large, ripe DOLE® Banana**
**1 cup DOLE® Strawberries**
**1 ripe DOLE® Mango, cubed**
**1 cup cranberry juice**
**1 cup ice cubes**

• Combine banana, strawberries, mango, juice and ice in blender or food processor container. Cover; blend until thick and smooth. *Makes 3 servings*

**Prep Time:** 10 minutes

# RASPBERRY SHERBET PUNCH

**1 to 2 liters HAWAIIAN PUNCH® Fruit Juicy Red**
**4 cups club soda**
**4 cups ginger ale**
**2 cups water**
**4 cups raspberry sherbet, divided**

Stir Hawaiian Punch, club soda, ginger ale, water and 2 cups sherbet in large punch bowl. Float remaining 2 cups sherbet in small scoops. *Makes 24 (6-ounce) servings*

## VIENNESE COFFEE

**1 cup heavy cream, divided**
**1 teaspoon powdered sugar**
**1 bar (3 ounces) bittersweet or semisweet chocolate**
**3 cups strong freshly brewed hot coffee**
**¼ cup crème de cacao or Irish cream (optional)**

1. Chill bowl, beaters and cream before whipping. Place ⅔ cup cream and sugar into chilled bowl. Beat with electric mixer at high speed until soft peaks form.

2. Cover and refrigerate up to 8 hours. If mixture has separated slightly after refrigeration, whisk lightly with wire whisk before using.

3. To make chocolate shavings for garnish, place waxed paper under chocolate. Holding chocolate in one hand, make short, quick strokes across chocolate with vegetable peeler; set aside. Break remaining chocolate into pieces.

4. Place remaining ⅓ cup cream in heavy small saucepan. Bring to a simmer over medium-low heat. Add chocolate pieces; cover and remove from heat. Let stand 5 minutes or until chocolate is melted; stir until smooth.

5. Add hot coffee to chocolate mixture. Heat over low heat just until bubbles form around edge of pan and coffee is heated through, stirring frequently. Remove from heat; stir in crème de cacao, if desired.

6. Pour into 4 warmed mugs. Top with whipped cream. Garnish with chocolate shavings.

*Makes about 4 (3½-cup) servings*

## FROSTY HOLIDAY GRAPES

**½ cup sugar**
**2 envelopes unflavored gelatin**
**10 small California grape clusters**
**Water**

Combine sugar and gelatin; mix well. Dip grape clusters in water; shake off excess water. Sprinkle sugar mixture through sieve over wet grapes. Place on waxed paper about 45 minutes or until dry.

*Makes 10 servings*

*Favorite recipe from **California Table Grape Commission***

## Express Recipe

Combine 8 ounces of softened cream cheese and ½ cup of your favorite preserves and mix well. Place in a medium serving bowl and serve with vanilla wafers.

# TACO POPCORN OLÉ

**9 cups air-popped popcorn**
**Butter-flavored cooking spray**
**1 teaspoon chili powder**
**½ teaspoon salt**
**½ teaspoon garlic powder**
**⅛ teaspoon ground red pepper (optional)**

1. Preheat oven to 350°F. Line 15×10-inch jelly-roll pan with foil.

2. Place popcorn in single layer in prepared pan. Coat lightly with cooking spray.

3. Combine chili powder, salt, garlic powder and red pepper, if desired, in small bowl; sprinkle over popcorn. Mix lightly to coat evenly.

4. Bake 5 minutes or until hot, stirring gently after 3 minutes. Spread mixture in single layer on large sheet of foil to cool.
*Makes 6 (1½-cup) servings*

TIP: Store popcorn mixture in tightly covered container at room temperature up to 4 days.

# HOLIDAY EGG NOG PUNCH

**2 (1-quart) cans BORDEN® Egg Nog, chilled**
**1 (12-ounce) can frozen orange juice concentrate, thawed**
**1 cup cold water**
**Orange sherbet**

1. In large pitcher combine all ingredients except sherbet; mix well.

2. Just before serving, pour into punch bowl; top with scoops of sherbet. Refrigerate leftovers.     *Makes about 1 quart*

**Prep Time:** 5 minutes

# CARAMEL-MARSHMALLOW APPLES

**1 package (14 ounces) caramels, unwrapped**
**1 cup miniature marshmallows**
**1 tablespoon water**
**5 or 6 small apples**

1. Line baking sheet with buttered waxed paper; set aside.

2. Combine caramels, marshmallows and water in medium saucepan. Cook over medium heat, stirring constantly, until caramels melt. Cool slightly while preparing apples.

3. Rinse and thoroughly dry apples. Insert flat sticks in stem ends of apples.

4. Dip each apple in caramel mixture, coating apples. Remove excess caramel mixture by scraping apple bottoms across rim of saucepan. Place on prepared baking sheet. Refrigerate until firm.                    *Makes 5 or 6 apples*

CARAMEL-NUT APPLES: Roll coated apples in chopped nuts before refrigerating.

CARAMEL-CHOCOLATE APPLES: Drizzle melted milk chocolate over coated apples before refrigerating.

# MANGO SMOOTHIE

**½ cup low-fat plain yogurt**
**1 ripe mango, peeled, seeded and sliced**
**¼ cup orange-pineapple juice**
**1 teaspoon honey**
**2 ice cubes**

Place all ingredients in blender container. Cover; blend until smooth. (Add milk if thinner consistency is desired.) Garnish with mint leaves, if desired.                    *Makes 1 serving*

## Express Recipe

For a quick kid-pleasing snack, dip chunks of banana in a combination of ½ cup creamy peanut butter and ⅓ cup milk. You can dip the coated banana chunks in miniature marshmallows, chopped peanuts or flaked coconut.

# SUNNY CITRUS FLOAT

½ **cup sweetened lemon-flavored iced tea mix**
1 **quart water**
⅓ **cup (3 ounces) frozen lemonade concentrate, thawed**
⅓ **can (3 ounces) frozen orange juice concentrate, thawed**
**Vanilla frozen yogurt**

Combine all ingredients except frozen yogurt in large pitcher. To serve, fill glasses about ⅔ full with iced tea mixture. Top each glass with 1 scoop frozen yogurt.

*Makes 4 to 6 servings*

# CHICKEN NUGGETS PARMIGIANA

1 **jar (1 pound 10 ounces) RAGÚ® Old World Style® Pasta Sauce**
1 **package (12 ounces) refrigerated or frozen fully-cooked chicken nuggets (about 18 nuggets)**
2 **cups shredded mozzarella cheese (about 8 ounces)**
1 **tablespoon grated Parmesan cheese**

1. Preheat oven to 375°F. In 13×9-inch baking dish, evenly spread 1½ cups Ragú Pasta Sauce. Arrange chicken nuggets in dish, top with remaining sauce and sprinkle with cheeses.

2. Cover with aluminum foil and bake 25 minutes. Remove foil and bake an additional 5 minutes.

*Makes 4 to 6 servings*

**Prep Time:** 5 minutes
**Cook Time:** 30 minutes

# SMOOTH MOCHA COFFEE

**¾ cup hot brewed coffee**
**2 tablespoons HERSHEY'S Syrup**
**Whipped cream (optional)**
**Ground cinnamon (optional)**

1. Stir together coffee and syrup in mug or cup. Garnish with whipped cream and cinnamon, if desired. Serve immediately.

*Makes 1 serving*

# VIRGIN PINEAPPLE COLADA

**1 cup DOLE® Pineapple Juice**
**1 cup crushed ice**
**1½ tablespoons sugar**
**1 tablespoon lime juice**
**½ teaspoon coconut extract**

• Combine pineapple juice, ice, sugar, lime juice and extract in blender container. Cover; blend until thick and smooth. Garnish with lime peel, if desired. Serve immediately.

*Makes 2 servings*

**Prep Time:** 10 minutes

# LIMEADE

**1 cup fresh lime juice (about 6 to 7 fresh limes)**
**4 cups cold water**
**⅔ cup sugar**
**Ice cubes**
**Lime slices**

Combine lime juice and water in large pitcher. Add sugar; stir until dissolved. Add ice cubes. Pour into glasses garnished with lime slices.

*Makes 6 servings*

NOTE: This recipe can also be adapted for fresh lemonade. Allow about six lemons to make 1 cup lemon juice.

## STRAWBERRY SPLASH PUNCH

**1½ cups fresh whole strawberries**
**½ cup lemon juice from concentrate, chilled**
**1 (14-ounce) can EAGLE BRAND® Sweetened Condensed Milk (NOT evaporated milk), chilled**
**1 (1-liter) bottle strawberry-flavored carbonated beverage, chilled**
**Ice cubes, if desired**
**Fresh whole strawberries, if desired**

1. In blender container, combine 1½ cups strawberries and lemon juice; cover and blend until smooth.

2. Add Eagle Brand; cover and blend. Pour into large pitcher. Gradually stir in carbonated beverage. Add ice, if desired. Garnish each serving with whole strawberry, if desired.

*Makes 10 servings*

**Prep Time:** 10 minutes

## TROPICAL STRAWBERRY FREEZE

**½ cup MAUNA LA'I® Paradise Passion® Juice Drink**
**¼ cup frozen strawberries, thawed**
**1½ tablespoons ROSE'S® Grenadine**
**1 cup crushed ice**
**Strawberry, for garnish**

Blend Mauna La'i Paradise Passion Juice Drink, strawberries, grenadine and ice in blender on high speed or until thoroughly combined. Pour into glass. Garnish with strawberry.

*Makes 1 drink*

## Express Recipe

Delight your kids with this snack mix. Place 1½ cups of sweetened corn and oat cereal and 1 cup teddy bear-shaped cookies on a jelly-roll pan. Spray with nonstick cooking spray and sprinkle with half of a mixture of 2 teaspoons sugar and ¾ teaspoon ground cinnamon. Stir well and bake in a preheated 350°F oven for 5 minutes. Stir in ½ cup dried fruit bits and 1 cup raisins. Spray with cooking spray and add the remaining sugar mixture. Stir well. Bake for 5 minutes more, then stir again. Serve at room temperature.

# PEANUT PITAS

**1 package (8 ounces) small pita breads, cut crosswise in half**
**16 teaspoons reduced-fat peanut butter**
**16 teaspoons strawberry spreadable fruit**
**1 large banana, peeled and thinly sliced (about 48 slices)**

1. Spread inside of each pita half with 1 teaspoon each peanut butter and spreadable fruit.

2. Fill pita halves evenly with banana slices. Serve immediately.
*Makes 8 servings*

HONEY BEES: Substitute honey for spreadable fruit.

JOLLY JELLIES: Substitute any flavor jelly for spreadable fruit and thin apple slices for banana slices.

P. B. CRUNCHERS: Substitute reduced-fat mayonnaise for spreadable fruit and celery slices for banana slices.

# CRANBERRY 'N' LEMON TEA PUNCH

**3 cups boiling water**
**6 tea bags**
**½ cup sugar**
**3 cups cranberry juice cocktail**
**¾ cup fresh squeezed lemon juice (juice of 4 to 5 SUNKIST® lemons)**
**Ice cubes**

In large pitcher, pour boiling water over tea bags. Cover and steep 5 minutes. Remove tea bags. Stir in sugar. Add cranberry and lemon juices; chill. Serve over ice. Garnish with lemon peel twists, if desired.
*Makes 7 (8-ounce) servings*

## CAPPUCCINO COOLER

**1½ cups cold coffee**
**1½ cups chocolate ice cream or frozen yogurt**
**¼ cup HERSHEY'S Syrup**
**Crushed ice**
**REDDI-WIP® Whipped Topping**
**Ground cinnamon (optional)**

• Place coffee, ice cream and HERSHEY'S Syrup in blender container. Cover; blend until smooth.

• Serve immediately over ice. Garnish with REDDI-WIP Whipped Topping and cinnamon.

*Makes about 4 (6-ounce) servings*

## HONEY LEMONADE WITH FROZEN FRUIT CUBES

**1½ cups lemon juice**
**¾ cup honey**
**9 cups water**
**48 small pieces assorted fruit**

Combine lemon juice and honey in large pitcher; stir until honey is dissolved. Stir in water. Place 1 to 2 pieces of fruit in each compartment of 2 ice cube trays. Fill each compartment with honey lemonade and freeze until firm. Chill remaining lemonade. To serve, divide frozen fruit cubes between tall glasses and fill with remaining lemonade.    *Makes 9 cups*

*Favorite recipe from **National Honey Board***

# FROZEN CHOCOLATE–COVERED BANANAS

**2 ripe medium bananas**
**4 wooden sticks**
**⅔ cup low-fat granola cereal without raisins**
**⅓ cup hot fudge sauce, at room temperature**

1. Line baking sheet or 15×10-inch jelly-roll pan with waxed paper; set aside.

2. Peel bananas; cut each in half crosswise. Insert wooden stick into center of cut end of each banana about 1½ inches into banana half. Place on prepared baking sheet; freeze until firm, at least 2 hours.

3. Place granola in large plastic food storage bag; crush slightly using rolling pin or meat mallet. Transfer granola to shallow plate. Place fudge sauce in a shallow dish.

4. Working with 1 banana at a time, place frozen banana in fudge sauce; turn banana and spread fudge sauce evenly onto banana with small rubber scraper. Immediately place banana on plate with granola; turn to coat lightly. Return to baking sheet in freezer. Repeat with remaining bananas.

5. Freeze until fudge sauce is very firm, at least 2 hours. Place on small plates; let stand 5 minutes before serving.

*Makes 4 servings*

# CHERRY SMOOTHIE

**2 cups frozen tart cherries**
**1 ripe banana, peeled**
**1 cup cherry juice blend**
**Maraschino cherries and pineapple chunks, for garnish**

Put frozen cherries, banana and cherry juice blend in container of electric blender or food processor. Purée until smooth. Pour into individual serving glasses. Garnish with maraschino cherries and pineapple, if desired. Serve immediately.

*Makes 4 (8-ounce) servings*

*Favorite recipe from **Cherry Marketing Institute***

## Express Recipe

For a no-bake cookie, combine 2 cups of crisp chow mein noodles, ½ cup cocktail peanuts and ⅓ cup raisins in a large bowl. Place ⅔ cup semisweet chocolate chips and ½ cup peanut butter chips in a medium microwavable bowl. Microwave at HIGH for 1 to 1½ minutes, stirring after 1 minute. Pour this mixture over the noodle mixture and stir until well coated. Drop the noodle mixture by tablespoonfuls onto waxed paper-lined baking sheets. Chill 1 hour or until the chocolate mixture is set. Store leftovers in an airtight container between sheets of waxed paper in the refrigerator.

# ORANGE SMOOTHIES

**1 cup vanilla ice cream or vanilla frozen yogurt
¾ cup milk
¼ cup frozen orange juice concentrate**

1. Combine ice cream, milk and orange juice concentrate in food processor or blender; process until smooth.

2. Pour mixture into 2 glasses; garnish as desired. Serve immediately.                     *Makes 2 servings*

# CHOCOLATE–PEANUT BUTTER–APPLE TREATS

**½ (8-ounce) package fat-free or reduced-fat cream cheese, softened
¼ cup reduced-fat chunky peanut butter
2 tablespoons mini chocolate chips
2 large apples**

1. Combine cream cheese, peanut butter and chocolate chips in a small bowl; mix well.

2. Cut each apple into 12 wedges; discard stems and seeds. Spread about 1½ teaspoons of the mixture over each apple wedge.                     *Makes 6 servings (4 apple wedges and 6 teaspoons spread)*

# FESTIVE STUFFED DATES

**1 box (8 ounces) DOLE® Whole Pitted Dates
1 package (3 ounces) reduced fat cream cheese, softened
¼ cup powdered sugar
1 tablespoon grated peel of 1 orange**

• Make slit in center of each date. Combine cream cheese, powdered sugar and orange peel. Fill centers of dates with cream cheese mixture. Refrigerate.

• Dust with additional powdered sugar just before serving, if desired.                     *Makes about 27 stuffed dates*

**Prep Time:** 25 minutes

## Express Recipe

For an Italian-inspired snack mix, combine 1½ cups Parmesan-flavored fish-shaped mini crackers, 1½ cups mini pretzels and 1 cup oyster crackers in a large bowl. Place 2 teaspoons butter, 1 teaspoon olive oil, 2 tablespoons grated Parmesan cheese, 1½ teaspoons Italian seasonings and ¼ teaspoon garlic powder in a small microwavable bowl. Microwave at MEDIUM for about 1 minute or just until the mixture is foamy. Pour this mixture over the pretzel mixture and toss until coated. Place in a 13×9-inch baking pan. Bake at 250°F for 15 minutes, stirring once.

## CHERRY S'MORES

**½ cup marshmallow creme**
**½ cup dried tart cherries**
**¼ cup semisweet chocolate chips**
**12 graham cracker squares (2½-inch squares)**

Combine marshmallow creme, cherries and chocolate chips; mix well. Place 6 of the graham crackers on microwave-safe plate. Spoon heaping tablespoon of marshmallow mixture on each cracker. Top with remaining crackers.

Microwave, uncovered, on HIGH (100%) 30 to 45 seconds, or until marshmallow mixture is soft and warm.

*Makes 6 servings*

NOTE: To prepare in conventional oven, place 6 of the graham crackers in an ovenproof baking dish. Proceed as above. Bake in a preheated 350°F oven 2 to 3 minutes, or until marshmallow mixture is soft and warm.

*Favorite recipe from **Cherry Marketing Institute***

## KAHLÚA® & COFFEE

**1½ ounces KAHLÚA® Liqueur**
**Hot coffee**
**Whipped cream (optional)**

Pour Kahlúa® into steaming cup of coffee. Top with whipped cream.

*Makes 1 serving*

# HONEY TEA COOLER

**1 pint fresh strawberries, stemmed and cleaned**
**¼ cup honey**
**1 can (6 ounces) frozen orange juice concentrate**
**2 cups brewed green tea, cooled**

In a blender or food processor container, combine strawberries and honey; process until smooth. Add orange juice concentrate; process until well blended. Stir into cooled tea. Serve over ice.                    *Makes 4 servings*

*Favorite recipe from **National Honey Board***

# ROASTED NUTS FROM HIDDEN VALLEY®

**1 pound assorted unsalted nuts, such as pecans,**
**    walnuts or mixed nuts**
**¼ cup maple syrup**
**2 tablespoons light brown sugar**
**1 packet (1 ounce) HIDDEN VALLEY® The Original Ranch®**
**    Salad Dressing & Seasoning Mix**

Place nuts in plastic bag; add maple syrup and coat well. Sprinkle sugar and salad dressing & seasoning mix over nuts. Coat well. Spread nuts in single layer on greased baking pan. Bake at 250°F for 35 minutes. Transfer immediately to large bowl. Cool, stirring to separate.          *Makes about 4 cups*

## Express Recipe

Cut a thawed pound cake into ½-inch slices, then into triangles. Spread each triangle with cream cheese frosting and sprinkle with toffee baking bits (or stir toffee bits into the frosting before spreading it on the pound cake).

## Quick Tip

Chavrie®, a cheese made from goat's milk, has a delicate flavor and a creamy texture. These characteristics make it great for snacking and for recipe use.

# CARAMEL POPCORN

**1 tablespoon margarine**
**1 cup packed light brown sugar**
**¼ cup water**
**6 cups air-popped popcorn**

1. Melt margarine in medium saucepan over medium heat. Add brown sugar and water; stir until sugar is dissolved. Bring to a boil; cover and cook 3 minutes.

2. Uncover pan; continue cooking mixture to the soft-crack stage (275°F on candy thermometer.) Do not overcook. Pour hot mixture over popcorn; stir with wooden spoon.

3. Spread popcorn in single layer on sheet of foil to cool. When cool, break apart.                    *Makes 6 (1-cup) servings*

# CHAVRIE® QUESADILLA

**½ cup drained cooked black beans**
**½ cup drained chunky tomato salsa**
**6 (6-inch) flour tortillas**
**1 (5.3-ounce) package CHAVRIE®, Plain or Basil**
**    & Roasted Garlic**
**2 teaspoons olive oil**

Combine black beans and salsa; spread onto 3 tortillas.

Lightly toast remaining 3 tortillas in oiled skillet.

Spread Chavrie onto toasted tortillas in skillet; place on top of black bean mixture to make "sandwich."

Add olive oil to skillet. Heat over medium heat until cheese starts to soften and tortilla starts to brown. Serve as is or cut into wedges.                    *Makes 6 servings*

# HOT CHOCOLATE

**3 ounces semisweet chocolate, finely chopped**
**¼ to ½ cup sugar**
**4 cups milk, divided**
**1 teaspoon vanilla**

Combine chocolate, sugar and ¼ cup milk in medium saucepan over medium-low heat. Cook, stirring constantly, until chocolate melts. Add remaining 3¾ cups milk; heat until hot, stirring occasionally. *Do not boil.* Remove from heat; stir in vanilla.

Beat with wire whisk until frothy. Pour into mugs and top with whipped cream or marshmallows, if desired. Serve immediately.                    *Makes 4 servings*

HOT COCOA: Substitute ¼ cup unsweetened cocoa powder for semisweet chocolate and use ½ cup sugar; heat as directed.

HOT MOCHA: Add 4 teaspoons instant coffee to milk mixture; heat as directed.

# CHOCOLATE NEW YORK EGG CREAM

**1 square (1 ounce) semisweet chocolate (optional)**
**¼ cup chocolate syrup**
**1 cup chilled club soda or carbonated mineral water**
**Ice**

Shave chocolate with vegetable peeler, if desired (makes about ½ cup).

Pour syrup into 12-ounce glass. Stir in club soda until foamy. Add ice. Garnish with 1 teaspoon chocolate shavings.* Serve immediately.                    *Makes 1 serving*

*\*Cover and refrigerate remaining chocolate shavings for another use.*

## Quick Tip

When cooking sugar syrups, take care because they can cause burns if they are splashed or spilled on the skin.

# SUGARED NUTS

**1 cup sugar**
**½ cup water**
**2½ cups unsalted mixed nuts**
**1 teaspoon vanilla**

Grease baking sheet; set aside.

Combine sugar and water in medium saucepan. Cook, stirring constantly, over medium heat until sugar dissolves.

Add nuts and vanilla. Cook, stirring occasionally, until water evaporates and nuts are sugary, about 12 minutes.

Spread on prepared baking sheet, separating nuts. Let stand until cooled.  *Makes about 1 pound*

# ORANGE–PINEAPPLE BREAKFAST SHAKE WITH YOGURT AND HONEY

**1 cup Florida orange or tangerine juice**
**½ cup unsweetened pineapple juice**
**½ cup plain low fat yogurt**
**1 teaspoon honey**
 **Orange twists or fresh mint leaves for garnish (optional)**

Add orange juice, pineapple juice, yogurt and honey to food processor or blender. Process until smooth. Pour into two glasses. Garnish with orange twists or fresh mint sprigs, if desired. Serve immediately.  *Makes 2 servings*

*Favorite recipe from **Florida Department of Citrus***

## BERRY–BANANA BREAKFAST SMOOTHIE

**1 carton (8 ounces) berry-flavored yogurt**
**1 ripe banana, cut into chunks**
**½ cup milk**

Place all ingredients in blender. Cover; blend until smooth.

*Makes about 2 cups*

## STUFFED BUNDLES

**1 package (10 ounces) refrigerated pizza dough**
**2 ounces lean ham or turkey ham, chopped**
**½ cup (2 ounces) shredded reduced-fat sharp**
    **Cheddar cheese**

1. Preheat oven to 425°F. Coat nonstick 12-cup muffin pan with nonstick cooking spray.

2. Unroll dough on flat surface; cut into 12 pieces, about 4×3 inch rectangles.

3. Divide ham and cheese between dough rectangles. Bring corners of dough together, pinching to seal. Place, smooth side up, in prepared muffin cups.

4. Bake 10 to 12 minutes or until golden.

*Makes 12 servings*

## MANGO–LIME COOLER

**2 large mangos, peeled, seeded and cubed**
**½ cup sugar**
**½ cup freshly squeezed lime juice (about 6 limes)**
**2 cups cold water**
**1 cup ice**

Combine all ingredients in blender. Blend at high speed until smooth.

*Makes 4 servings*

# Marinades, Sauces & More

## Express Recipe

Combine 1 cup mayonnaise, 2 cloves minced garlic and 1¼ teaspoons dill weed. Use this mixture as a dipping sauce for cut-up vegetables or chicken nuggets.

## HOT FUDGE SAUCE

**1 (6-ounce) package semi-sweet chocolate chips (1 cup)**
  ***or* 4 (1-ounce) squares semi-sweet chocolate**
**2 tablespoons butter or margarine**
**1 (14-ounce) can EAGLE BRAND® Sweetened Condensed Milk (NOT evaporated milk)**
**2 tablespoons water**
**1 teaspoon vanilla extract**

1. In heavy saucepan over medium heat, melt chips and butter with Eagle Brand and water. Cook and stir constantly until smooth. Stir in vanilla.

2. Serve warm over ice cream or as dipping sauce for fruit. Refrigerate leftovers. *Makes 2 cups sauce*

MICROWAVE DIRECTIONS: In 1-quart glass measure, combine ingredients. Microwave at HIGH (100% power) 3 to 3½ minutes, stirring after each minute. Proceed as directed above.

TO REHEAT: In small heavy saucepan, combine desired amount of Hot Fudge Sauce with small amount of water. Over low heat, stir constantly until heated through.

SPIRITED HOT FUDGE SAUCE: Add ¼ cup almond, coffee, mint or orange-flavored liqueur with vanilla.

**Prep Time: 10 minutes**

*Left to right:* HOT FUDGE SAUCE
AND DULCE DE LECHE (PAGE 272)

# SPICED PEACH SAUCE

**2 pounds frozen sliced unsweetened peaches, thawed**
**2 cups sugar**
**1½ teaspoons lemon juice**
**1½ teaspoons ground cinnamon**
**¼ teaspoon ground nutmeg**

1. Combine peaches and thawing liquid, sugar, lemon juice, cinnamon and nutmeg in heavy, medium saucepan.

2. Bring to a boil over high heat. Boil 45 to 50 minutes or until thickened, stirring occasionally and breaking peaches into small pieces with back of wooden spoon. Remove saucepan from heat; cool completely.

3. Store in airtight container in refrigerator up to 2 months. Serve with waffles, pancakes or French toast.

*Makes about 3 cups*

# FRESH TOMATO–BASIL SALSA

**1 pound fresh tomatoes, peeled and seeded**
**½ cup loosely packed fresh basil leaves**
**¼ small onion (about 2×1-inch piece)**
**1 teaspoon red wine vinegar**
**¼ teaspoon salt**

Combine ingredients in food processor; process until finely chopped but not smooth.     *Makes about 1 cup*

# SMUCKER'S® LEMON APRICOT MARINADE

**½ cup SMUCKER'S® Apricot Preserves**
**¼ cup pitted green olives, sliced into quarters**
**Juice and grated peel of 1 large lemon (about**
  **3 tablespoons juice and 1 tablespoon peel)**
**1 teaspoon freshly ground black pepper**
**¼ teaspoon salt**

Combine all ingredients in a small bowl and mix well. Use marinade for grilling and basting shrimp, salmon, swordfish or chicken.     *Makes 6 servings*

## SWEET 'N' SMOKY BBQ SAUCE

**½ cup ketchup**
**⅓ cup *French's*® Bold n' Spicy Brown Mustard**
**⅓ cup light molasses**
**¼ cup *French's*® Worcestershire Sauce**
**¼ teaspoon liquid smoke or hickory salt (optional)**

Combine ketchup, mustard, molasses, Worcestershire and liquid smoke, if desired, in medium bowl. Mix until well blended. Brush on chicken or ribs during last 15 minutes of grilling.              *Makes about 1½ cups sauce*

**Prep Time:** 5 minutes

## PEANUT BUTTER CHOCOLATE SAUCE

**1 (7-ounce) pure milk chocolate candy bar**
**½ cup 2% milk**
**½ cup peanut butter**
**1 teaspoon vanilla extract**

Break chocolate into small pieces and place in a small bowl. In a small saucepan, heat milk until bubbles appear at the edge (do not boil). Pour milk over chocolate. Let sit 3 minutes; stir until chocolate is melted. Add peanut butter and vanilla; stir until smooth and glossy.              *Makes 6 servings*

*Favorite recipe from **Peanut Advisory Board***

## CREAMY GINGER SPREAD

**1 package (3 ounces) cream cheese, at room temperature**
**2 tablespoons butter or margarine**
**2 tablespoons honey or pineapple preserves**
**⅛ teaspoon ground ginger**

Fit processor with steel blade. Process ingredients 20 to 30 seconds or until well blended. Serve as a spread for quick breads and muffins.              *Makes about ⅔ cup*

---

## Express Recipe

For an easy pineapple salsa, combine 2 cups chopped pineapple with ½ cup finely chopped sweet onion, ¼ cup pineapple juice, 2 teaspoons chopped fresh mint, and finely chopped and minced jalapeño pepper to taste. Serve with grilled chicken or fish.

## CHOCO-HOT SAUCE

**1 cup semisweet chocolate chips**
**⅓ cup sugar**
**⅓ cup water**
**2 tablespoons butter**
**1½ teaspoons TABASCO® brand Pepper Sauce**

Combine chocolate chips, sugar, water and butter in small saucepan over medium heat; heat just to boiling, stirring constantly. Remove from heat; stir in TABASCO® Sauce. Serve warm over ice cream, cake or fruit.          *Makes 1 cup sauce*

## FAJITA MARINADE

**½ cup lime juice *or* ¼ cup lime juice and ¼ cup tequila or beer**
**1 tablespoon minced garlic**
**1 tablespoon dried oregano leaves**
**2 teaspoons ground cumin**
**2 teaspoons black pepper**

Combine lime juice, garlic, oregano, cumin and black pepper in 1-cup glass measure. Use to marinate beef or chicken for fajitas.          *Makes ⅔ cup*

## HONEY PRALINE SAUCE

**¾ cup pecan halves**
**2 tablespoons butter or margarine**
**½ cup honey**
**1 teaspoon all-purpose flour**
**⅓ cup whipping cream**

Preheat oven to 300°F. Spread pecans in shallow pan. Bake in 15 minutes. Melt butter in small saucepan over medium heat. Blend in honey, flour and dash salt. Reduce heat to low and simmer 5 minutes, stirring constantly. Remove from heat and let cool. Blend in cream, stirring until smooth. Stir in pecans.
          *Makes 1½ cups*

TIP: Serve over ice cream or as a topping for baked apples, poached pears or peaches.

---

## Express Recipe

Combine ½ cup melted butter or margarine, ¼ cup Dijon mustard and 1½ teaspoons lemon-pepper seasoning. Serve with fish or chicken.

## SOUTHWEST SALSA DRESSING

**⅔ cup mild salsa***
**2 tablespoons plain nonfat yogurt**
**4 teaspoons sugar**
**2 teaspoons chopped fresh cilantro (optional)**

*\*For a hotter and spicier dressing, use medium or hot salsa.*

In a small bowl stir all ingredients together. Or, blend ingredients in a food processor for a smoother dressing. Chill or serve immediately over green salad, chicken or turkey salad, taco salad or seafood salad.            *Makes 4 servings*

*Favorite recipe from **The Sugar Association, Inc.***

## CHUTNEY GLAZE

**1 cup PATAK'S® Major Grey Mango Chutney**
**2 tablespoons Dijon mustard**

In small bowl, combine chutney and mustard. Baste on chicken or pork before grilling or broiling.

*Makes about 1 cup glaze*

## STRAWBERRY SAUCE

**1 box (10 ounces) BIRDS EYE® frozen Strawberries, thawed**
**1 tablespoon sugar**
**2 teaspoons cornstarch**
**1 teaspoon lemon juice**

• Drain strawberries, reserving syrup. Combine 1 tablespoon strawberry syrup with sugar and cornstarch in saucepan; stir until smooth.

• Add remaining syrup, strawberries and lemon juice; bring to boil over medium heat, stirring frequently.

• Cook until sauce thickens and is translucent. Serve warm over pancakes, waffles or ice cream.            *Makes 1½ cups*

**Prep Time:** 2 minutes
**Cook Time:** 8 to 10 minutes

## Express Recipe

Combine ½ cup melted butter, 2 teaspoons grated lemon or lime peel and ¼ cup lemon or lime juice. Serve this mixture as a simple sauce for fish or chicken.

## Express Recipe

Make a quick pan sauce for chicken by adding ½ cup lemon or other citrus juice to a skillet after cooking chicken. Cook for 1 minute, scraping up any brown bits in the pan. Add 1 cup chicken broth and 1 tablespoon mustard. Cook and stir until slightly thickened.

## CITRUS BUTTER

**1 cup butter, softened**
**¾ teaspoon grated orange peel**
**2 tablespoons fresh orange juice**
**¼ teaspoon lime peel**

1. Combine butter, orange peel, orange juice and lime peel in medium bowl with electric mixer. Beat at medium speed until well blended.

2. Place butter mixture on sheet of waxed paper. Using waxed paper to hold butter mixture, roll it back and forth to form a log. Wrap log in plastic wrap.

3. Store in airtight container in refrigerator up to 2 weeks.

*Makes about 1 cup*

SERVING NOTE: Remove desired amount from roll; immediately refrigerate remaining butter.

HONEY BUTTER: Omit orange peel, orange juice and lime peel. Substitute ¼ cup honey.

STRAWBERRY BUTTER: Omit orange peel, orange juice and lime peel. Substitute ⅔ cup strawberry preserves.

## ORIGINAL RANCH® TARTAR SAUCE

**1 packet (1 ounce) HIDDEN VALLEY® The Original Ranch® Salad Dressing & Seasoning Mix**
**⅓ cup mayonnaise**
**⅓ cup sour cream**
**2 tablespoons sweet pickle relish**

Remove 1 tablespoon salad dressing & seasoning mix from packet; reserving remaining mix for another use. Blend mix with mayonnaise, sour cream and pickle relish. Chill 1 hour before serving.

*Makes about 1 cup*

## *Express Recipe*

To make a quick mango salsa for chicken, combine the diced fruit from 2 mangos with the juice of 2 limes, 2 tablespoons chopped fresh cilantro, 2 teaspoons *each* minced garlic and minced jalapeño pepper to taste.

## EASY HONEY MUSTARD BARBECUE SAUCE

**1 bottle (10.5 ounces) PLOCHMAN'S® Mild Yellow Mustard (about 1 cup)**
**½ cup barbecue sauce**
**¼ cup honey**
**2 tablespoons finely minced onion**

Mix all ingredients in medium bowl. Use as a condiment, or brush on chicken, pork chops or seafood.          *Makes 2 cups*

**Prep Time:** 5 minutes

## SWEET ADOBO SAUCE

**2 to 3 whole chipotle peppers in adobo sauce, finely chopped**
**½ teaspoon fresh minced garlic**
**1 jar (10 ounces) KNOTT'S BERRY FARM® Raspberry Preserves or Apricot & Pineapple Preserves**
**½ tablespoon cider vinegar**

In small saucepan over medium heat, sauté chipotle peppers and garlic until garlic is tender; stir constantly. Add preserves and vinegar. Bring to a boil; reduce heat and simmer 5 minutes. Serve warm over baked ham, pork chops or chicken.

*Makes 1¾ cups sauce*

**Prep Time:** 10 minutes

## HORSERADISH SAUCE

**1 cup fat-free sour cream**
**¼ cup finely chopped fresh parsley**
**1 tablespoon prepared horseradish**
**1 tablespoon Dijon mustard**
**½ teaspoon salt**

Combine all ingredients in small bowl until well blended.

*Makes about 1¼ cups*

**The publisher would like to thank the companies and organizations listed below for the use of their recipes and photographs in this publication.**

Alouette® Cheese

Barilla America, Inc.

BelGioioso® Cheese, Inc.

Birds Eye®

Bob Evans®

Butterball® Turkey

California Table Grape Commission

Chef Paul Prudhomme's Magic Seasoning Blends®

Cherry Marketing Institute

ConAgra Foods®

Del Monte Corporation

Dole Food Company, Inc.

Dreyer's / Edy's Grand Ice Cream

Duncan Hines® and Moist Deluxe® are registered trademarks of Aurora Foods Inc.

Eagle Brand®

Filippo Berio® Olive Oil

Fleischmann's® Margarines and Spreads

Florida Department of Agriculture and Consumer Services, Bureau of Seafood and Aquaculture

Florida's Citrus Growers

The Golden Grain Company®

Grandma's® is a registered trademark of Mott's, Inc.

Guiltless Gourmet®

Hawaiian Punch® is a registered trademark of Mott's, Inc.

Hershey Foods Corporation

The Hidden Valley® Food Products Company

Hillshire Farm®

Holland House® is a registered trademark of Mott's, Inc.

Hormel Foods, LLC

Idaho Potato Commission

Kahlúa® Liqueur

Keebler® Company

The Kingsford Products Company

Lawry's® Foods

Lee Kum Kee (USA) Inc.

© Mars, Incorporated 2004

Mauna La'i® is a registered trademark of Mott's, Inc.

McIlhenny Company (TABASCO® brand Pepper Sauce)

Mrs. Dash®

National Cherry Growers & Industries Foundation

National Honey Board

National Pork Board

Nestlé USA

Norseland, Inc. Lucini Italia Co.

Ortega®

Peanut Advisory Board

Perdue Farms Incorporated

Plochman, Inc.

Reckitt Benckiser Inc.

Reddi-wip® is a registered trademark of ConAgra Brands, Inc.

Riviana Foods Inc.

The J.M. Smucker Company

Sonoma® Dried Tomatoes

Southeast United Dairy Industry Association, Inc.

The Sugar Association, Inc.

Reprinted with permission of Sunkist Growers, Inc.

Uncle Ben's Inc.

Unilever Bestfoods North America

Walnut Marketing Board

Washington Apple Commission

Wisconsin Milk Marketing Board

# METRIC CONVERSION CHART

## VOLUME MEASUREMENTS (dry)

$1/8$ teaspoon = 0.5 mL
$1/4$ teaspoon = 1 mL
$1/2$ teaspoon = 2 mL
$3/4$ teaspoon = 4 mL
1 teaspoon = 5 mL
1 tablespoon = 15 mL
2 tablespoons = 30 mL
$1/4$ cup = 60 mL
$1/3$ cup = 75 mL
$1/2$ cup = 125 mL
$2/3$ cup = 150 mL
$3/4$ cup = 175 mL
1 cup = 250 mL
2 cups = 1 pint = 500 mL
3 cups = 750 mL
4 cups = 1 quart = 1 L

## VOLUME MEASUREMENTS (fluid)

1 fluid ounce (2 tablespoons) = 30 mL
4 fluid ounces ($1/2$ cup) = 125 mL
8 fluid ounces (1 cup) = 250 mL
12 fluid ounces ($1 1/2$ cups) = 375 mL
16 fluid ounces (2 cups) = 500 mL

## WEIGHTS (mass)

$1/2$ ounce = 15 g
1 ounce = 30 g
3 ounces = 90 g
4 ounces = 120 g
8 ounces = 225 g
10 ounces = 285 g
12 ounces = 360 g
16 ounces = 1 pound = 450 g

## DIMENSIONS

$1/16$ inch = 2 mm
$1/8$ inch = 3 mm
$1/4$ inch = 6 mm
$1/2$ inch = 1.5 cm
$3/4$ inch = 2 cm
1 inch = 2.5 cm

## OVEN TEMPERATURES

250°F = 120°C
275°F = 140°C
300°F = 150°C
325°F = 160°C
350°F = 180°C
375°F = 190°C
400°F = 200°C
425°F = 220°C
450°F = 230°C

## BAKING PAN SIZES

| Utensil | Size in Inches/Quarts | Metric Volume | Size in Centimeters |
|---|---|---|---|
| Baking or Cake Pan (square or rectangular) | 8×8×2 | 2 L | 20×20×5 |
| | 9×9×2 | 2.5 L | 23×23×5 |
| | 12×8×2 | 3 L | 30×20×5 |
| | 13×9×2 | 3.5 L | 33×23×5 |
| Loaf Pan | 8×4×3 | 1.5 L | 20×10×7 |
| | 9×5×3 | 2 L | 23×13×7 |
| Round Layer Cake Pan | 8×1½ | 1.2 L | 20×4 |
| | 9×1½ | 1.5 L | 23×4 |
| Pie Plate | 8×1¼ | 750 mL | 20×3 |
| | 9×1¼ | 1 L | 23×3 |
| Baking Dish or Casserole | 1 quart | 1 L | — |
| | 1½ quart | 1.5 L | — |
| | 2 quart | 2 L | — |